MODERN LEGAL STUDIES

SECURITY OF TENURE UNDER THE RENT ACT

AUSTRALIA AND NEW ZEALAND
The Law Book Company Ltd.
Sydney : Melbourne : Perth

CANADA AND U.S.A
The Carswell Company Ltd.
Agincourt, Ontario

INDIA
N. M. Tripathi Private Ltd.
Bombay
and
Eastern Law House Private Ltd.
Calcutta and Delhi
M.P.P. House
Bangalore

ISRAEL
Steimatzky's Agency Ltd.
Jerusalem : Tel Aviv : Haifa

MALAYSIA : SINGAPORE : BRUNEI
Malayan Law Journal (Pte.) Ltd.
Singapore and Kuala Lumpur

PAKISTAN
Pakistan Law House
Karachi

MODERN LEGAL STUDIES

SECURITY OF TENURE UNDER THE RENT ACT

by

JILL E. MARTIN, LL.M. (Lond.)
Reader in Law,
King's College London

LONDON
SWEET & MAXWELL
1986

Published in 1986 by
Sweet & Maxwell Limited of
11 New Fetter Lane, London.
Computerset by Promenade Graphics Limited, Cheltenham.
Printed in Great Britain by
Page Bros. (Norwich) Limited.

British Library Cataloguing in Publication Data

Martin, Jill E.
   Security of tenure under the rent act.—
   (Modern legal studies)
   1. Rental housing—Law and legislation—
   England
   I. Title   II. Series
   344.2064'344   KD899

   ISBN 0–421–36330–4
   ISBN 0–421–36340–1 Pbk

PREFACE

1985 seemed a good year to write a book about the Rent Act. First, it marked the seventieth anniversary of the original legislation in 1915. Secondly, five years had passed since the last substantial revision of the Rent Act by the Housing Act 1980, a period sufficient to make feasible some assessment of the merits of its reforms. Thirdly, 1985 was the year in which the case of *Street* v. *Mountford* was decided by the House of Lords. That decision, on the distinction between leases and licences, plainly has a not insignificant effect upon the operation of the Rent Act. In the same year other decisions of the House of Lords in this field were reported, notably *Hampstead Way Investments Ltd.* v. *Lewis-Weare*, on the "two homes" tenant, and *Lewis* v. *Lewis* on the transfer of the statutory tenancy on divorce. These decisions, plus many others in the lower courts, coupled with the Rent (Amendment) Act 1985, set the scene for a new review of the Rent Act 1977. 1985 was also the year during which the Conservative Government withdrew a proposal for the decontrol of new lettings. It seems that no major amendment to the Rent Act will be enacted during the life of the present Government. What happens thereafter depends, of course, on the outcome of the next general election, but there is little chance of any legislation which would take away existing protection.

This book has been written primarily for students of landlord and tenant law, at both undergraduate and postgraduate levels. It is hoped that it might also be of use to practitioners and others who need to know the workings of the legislation. Basic property law textbooks, and even general landlord and tenant textbooks, cannot devote space to a thorough treatment of the Rent Act. The aim has been to fill the gap which exists between those books and the very detailed treatment of the topic in the specialist practitioners' books. It is hoped that the reader will here find a critical account of the Act and the case-law upon it which is thorough but not too technical in its approach.

All the major aspects of security and rent control have been dealt with, but space has not permitted an exhaustive survey of the entire contents of the legislation. For this reason the provisions relating to agricultural workers, mortgages, housing trusts and housing associations have been omitted, along with other miscellaneous matters not regarded as within the mainstream of the Rent Act.

My intention has been to state the law as at January 1, 1986.

December 31, 1985   Jill Martin
                                                 King's College London

CONTENTS

OTHER BOOKS IN THE SERIES

TABLE OF CASES

TABLE OF STATUTES

TABLE OF STATUTORY INSTRUMENTS

Chapter 1

INTRODUCTION

The Rent Acts have been with us now for 70 years. This brief his-
torical survey will show a story of piecemeal amendment and consolidation, with major legislation following a change of
government, only to be reversed by a subsequent change of
government.

As a temporary wartime measure, the Increase of Rent and
Mortgage Interest (War Restrictions) Act was passed in 1915. At
this time a far greater proportion of the population lived in private
rented accommodation than is the case today,[1] with the growth of
the public sector and owner occupation. Other Acts followed in
the remaining years of the First World War. However, the end of
the war did not bring with it any decrease in the housing shortage.
The legislation was consolidated in 1920 by the Increase of Rent
and Mortgage Interest (Restrictions) Act, which brought more
properties into control by raising the rateable value limits. This
Act, as its name suggests, restricted rents and the rates of mortgage interest and conferred security of tenure.

A measure of decontrol followed in the period between the wars
as a result of legislation in 1923, 1933 and 1938, but this trend was
reversed by the Rent and Mortgage Interest Restrictions Act 1939.
The Acts of 1920 and 1939 dealt with what were known as "controlled tenancies," and survived until the consolidating legislation
of 1968.

None of the legislation so far mentioned gave protection to furnished lettings. A separate code of protection for them was introduced by the Furnished Houses (Rent Control) Act 1946, creating
rent tribunals having jurisdiction to fix the rent and to confer a
measure of security of tenure.[2]

The Conservative Government introduced significant decontrol
in the Rent Act 1957, but most of the properties decontrolled by
that Act were brought back into protection on a change of government by the Rent Act 1965, which introduced "regulated tenancies" and a new system of rent control involving the registration

---

[1] Today's figure is under 10 per cent; (1985) 274 E.G. 1074; Murphy and
Clark, *The Family Home*, Chap. 1.
[2] This was amended by the Landlord and Tenant (Rent Control) Act
1949. The Housing Repairs and Rent Act 1954 permitted rent to be
increased to reflect repairs, to encourage the latter.

of "fair rents," assessed by the rent officer, with an appeal to the rent assessement committee.

This was followed by the consolidating Rent Act 1968, which included (in Part VI) the provisions on furnished lettings. These were known as "Part VI contracts" (and are now called "restricted contracts").

The Housing Act 1969 provided for the conversion of some controlled tenancies to regulated tenancies provided the property had the standard amenities and was in good repair. This was replaced by the Housing Finance Act 1972, a Conservative measure, which extended this process by providing for the phased conversion of all controlled tenancies into regulated tenancies according to their rateable values. However, a return to power by the Labour Party put an end to this process in the Housing Rents and Subsidies Act 1975.

The Labour Government introduced a major reform in the Rent Act 1974, bringing furnished lettings into full protection and excluding tenants of resident landlords. These tenants received the limited protection of the restricted contract code which had previously applied to furnished lettings.

Another consolidation followed in the Rent Act 1977, the current Act.[3] This Act, like its predecessors, reveals the legislative method of simply lifting sections from previous Acts, sometimes without regard to their appropriateness to modern conditions. So, for example section 101, dealing with overcrowding, was stated to apply only to premises "used as a separate dwelling by members of the working classes or of a type suitable for such use."[3a]

The Conservative Government returned to its policy of abolishing controlled tenancies in the Housing Act 1980. Those that remained were converted to regulated tenancies (or, if there was any business use, to tenancies within Part II of the Landlord and Tenant Act 1954). This affected approximately 200,000 properties.[4] A major feature of the 1980 Act was the introduction of the security of tenure and the right to buy for local authority tenants. These provisions, now found in the Housing Act 1985, are outside the scope of this book, but other significant changes brought about by the Act in the private sector included the creation of shorthold and assured tenancies[5] and the reduction of the limited security of tenure enjoyed by tenants within the restricted contract code.

---

[3] As amended by the Housing Act 1980. The Act does not apply to Scotland or Northern Ireland.
[3a] The reference to the working classes was finally deleted by the Housing (Consequential Provisions) Act 1985, Sched. 2.
[4] See (1980) 253 E.G. 125.
[5] *Post*, p. 45.

The most recent legislation is the Rent (Amendment) Act 1985, which simply amends the requirements of one of the grounds for possession.[6]

The general scheme of the current legislation is to provide security of tenure to the tenant and his family, subject to grounds for possession established by the landlord, and to provide financial security by controlling the rent level, coupled with a prohibition on premiums. This, then, is the statutory protection for people who must look to the private rented sector because they do not qualify for local authority housing but cannot afford to be owner occupiers. The need for such legislation, of course, arises from the fact that the demand for such accommodation exceeds the supply. The legislation is, however, to some extent the cause of the shortage, as strict controls result in many landlords preferring to sell their property when it falls vacant, rather than re-let.

Finally, a recent review of the Rent Acts by the Department of the Environment proposed that, while security for present tenants should continue, control should cease in respect of new lettings. This, it was hoped, would encourage letting and thereby ease the shortage of rental accommodation.[7] Under threats by the Labour Party to repeal any such legislation, however, it has been decided not to include the proposals in the 1985/86 legislative programme.[8]

Other Codes of Statutory Protection

Before considering the Rent Act in detail, it will be convenient to mention briefly certain other types of statutory protection, relating to both residential and non-residential tenancies.

Agricultural tenancies (which may be partly residential) fall within the protection of the Agricultural Holdings Act 1948, as amended, which gives security of tenure, subject to grounds for possession. Business tenancies, including those which are mixed business and residential, are protected by the Landlord and Tenant Act 1954, Part II. This gives security of tenure, subject to grounds for possession, while leaving the rent subject to market forces.

In the residential sphere, it has already been noted that public

---

[6] The Act was passed to reverse *Pocock* v. *Steel* [1985] 1 W.L.R. 229, *post*, p. 83.

[7] Local authorities have estimated that in April 1985 there were 545,000 empty homes in the private sector in England, of which 100,000 were in London; *The Times*, February 21, 1986. Typical examples are flats above shops.

[8] See (1985) 274 E.G. 1074, *The Times*, February 21, 1986.

sector tenants were given security of tenure and the right to buy by the Housing Act of 1980.[9] The "fair rent" system, however, does not apply. These are called "secure tenancies." Long leases (meaning those exceeding 21 years at a low rent, a premium having been paid) are protected primarily by Part I of the Landlord and Tenant Act 1954 which, on termination of the tenancy, provides security of tenure in similar manner to the Rent Act. In addition, long leaseholders of houses (as opposed to flats) are given the right to buy the freehold at a favourable price (or to renew the lease for 50 years) by the Leasehold Reform Act 1967. This is subject to a residence requirement, and to grounds of opposition by the landlord (where, however, compensation must be paid to the tenant). Finally, the Rent (Agriculture) Act 1976 gives security of tenure, which is broadly similar to that conferred by the Rent Act, to agricultural workers housed by their employers.

The tenant's degree of protection, which varies from code to code, can be assessed by considering how many of the following features are included:

(a) *Security of tenure.* This is the fundamental feature, but it does not, however, apply to restricted contracts under the Rent Act 1977. One aspect is the question of whether compensation is payable by the landlord on establishing a ground for possession which is not based on the tenant's default. This is the case with business, agricultural and assured tenancies, but not with Rent Act or public sector secure tenancies.

(b) *Succession rights.* Does the original tenant's security continue beyond his death in favour of his family? This is the case with private sector tenancies under the Rent Act (for two generations), public sector tenancies under the Housing Act (for one generation), and agricultural holdings (but restricted to existing lettings by the Agricultural Holdings Act 1984).

(c) *Rent control.* This is a common feature, for example, "fair rents" under the Rent Act 1977. This system, however, does not apply to public sector tenancies, nor to business tenancies (where the market rent is recoverable).

(d) *Control of other terms of the tenancy.* For example, assign-

---

[9] Now the Act of 1985. This Act also deals with tenants of Housing Trusts and Housing Associations (see s.80). Basically such tenancies are within the "secure tenancy" code but the rent is governed by the Rent Act 1977.

ment may be prohibited, as with statutory tenancies under
the Rent Act and secure tenancies under the Housing Act.

(e) *The right to buy the freehold* (or to acquire a long lease).
This is the scheme , as stated above, for long leaseholders
of houses under the Leasehold Reform Act 1967. Similarly
in the case of public sector secure tenants, whether of
houses or flats (the acquisition of a long lease being the only
possibility in the latter case).

(f) *Is contracting out possible?* This is clearly prohibited by
some Acts (for example, the Agricultural Holdings legislation, the Leasehold Reform Act 1967 and, as a general
rule, the Landlord and Tenant Act 1954, Part II). In the
case of the Rent Act, we will see that contracting out is not
permitted by the courts, although there is no express statutory prohibition. Subject to certain safeguards, a measure
of contracting out is permitted, however, by an amendment
to the 1954 Act (business tenancies).[10]

(g) *Are licensees included?* The general position is that tenancies are protected, not licences. The Rent Act contains a
limited exception in that licensees can come within the
restricted contract code. Certain licensees are also protected by the Agricultural Holdings Act, the Housing Act
1985 (public sector) and the Rent (Agriculture) Act 1976.

The Protection from Eviction Act 1977

To complete the picture mention should be made of the protection
afforded to residential tenants (and certain licensees) by this Act.
In the case of certain residential occupiers excluded from the Rent
Act, this will be their only source of statutory protection.

The provisions were originally contained in Part III of the Rent
Act 1965 (which followed the temporary Protection from Eviction
Act 1964). These sections, and section 16 of the Rent Act 1957,
were consolidated by the 1977 Act, which has subsequently been
amended by the Housing Act 1980.

Section 1 provides for the criminal offence[11] of unlawful eviction
and harassment. Under section 1(2),[12] it is an offence if any person

---

[10] L.T.A. 1954, s.38(4), introduced by Law of Property Act 1969, s.5.

[11] By s.1(4), the punishment is fine or imprisonment, or both.

[12] See *R.* v. *Yuthiwattana* [1984] Crim.L.R. 562. The offence under s.1(2)
must have the character of eviction. This need not be permanent, but
locking the tenant out overnight would not suffice, s.1(3) being more
appropriate in such a case.

unlawfully deprives the residential occupier of his occupation, or attempts to do so, unless he proves that he believed (with reasonable cause) that the occupier had ceased to reside in the premises.

By section 1(3),[13] it is an offence if any person, with intent to cause the residential occupier to give up occupation or to refrain from exercising his rights, does acts calculated to interfere with the peace or comfort of the occupier or members of his household, or persistently withdraws or withholds services reasonably required for the occupation of the premises.

A "residential occupier" means, by section 1(1), a person occupying the premises as a residence, whether under a contract or by virtue of any enactment or rule of law giving him the right to remain in occupation or restricting the right of any other person to recover possession. This definition, therefore, includes both tenants and contractual licensees,[14] whether or not they are protected by the Rent Act.

There is no civil action under this section for damages.[15] By section 1(5), however, nothing in the section prejudices any liability or remedy to which the person guilty of an offence may be subject in civil proceedings. It is likely that the facts that give rise to the commission of an offence under the section will also found civil liability, for example, for the tort of trespass or for breach of the covenant for quiet enjoyment.[16]

It has been held that a person accused of an offence under section 1(3) has a defence if he honestly believed, with reasonable grounds, that the occupant was not a "residential occupier."[17]

Section 2 provides that the right to forfeit a lease of a dwelling cannot lawfully be enforced other than by court proceedings while any person is lawfully residing in the premises. This provision is significant for those tenants who are not within the Rent Act. Forfeiture of a protected tenancy, as we will see, does not automati-

---

[13] *Ibid.* Harassment under s.1(3) need not breach the right of occupation. The offence was committed by refusing to supply a key when the tenant's was missing.

[14] Unless the licence has been effectively terminated; *R.* v. *Blankley* [1979] Crim L.R. 166. Former unprotected tenants are within the definition in cases where the landlord's right to possession may not be enforced without a court order under s.3 (*infra*) or, in cases of forfeiture, under s.2 (*infra*). See also Criminal Law Act 1977, s.6.

[15] *McCall* v. *Abelesz* [1976] Q.B. 585; *cf. Warder* v. *Cooper* [1970] 1 Ch. 495 (on what is now s.3 of the 1977 Act).

[16] See *Drane* v. *Evangelou* [1978] 1 W.L.R. 455 (exemplary damages).

[17] *R.* v. *Phekoo* [1981] 1 W.L.R. 1117. The requirement of reasonable grounds is criticised at [1981] Conv. 377 (M. Wasik). The question could also arise under s.1(2).

cally entitle the landlord to possession, and a court order based on a Rent Act ground for possession must be obtained.[18]

Section 3 prohibits eviction without a court order where premises have been let as a dwelling and the occupier continues to reside in the premises after the tenancy has come to an end (*e.g.* by expiry or notice to quit). This section applies only to a tenancy which is not "statutorily protected,"[19] and provides, therefore, a minimum protection for residential tenants outside the Rent Act. It applies also to tenancies which are restricted contracts within the Rent Act 1977.

Although primarily concerned with tenancies, section 3 also protects two kinds of licensee. First, a service occupier with exclusive possession[20]; and, a secondly, a licensee who has a restricted contract within the meaning of the Rent Act.[21] The reason for this is that the scheme of the Housing Act 1980 for the protection of restricted contracts is that the court has a discretion to suspend a possession order for up to three months. It is essential, therefore, to the working of this scheme that restricted contracts, whether tenancies or licences, cannot be terminated without a court order.

By section 3(2), "the occupier" means any person lawfully residing at the termination of the former tenancy. Questions may arise, both here and under section 2, as to what is meant by "lawfully residing." It is not clear whether a sub-tenant whose sub-lease is in breach of a covenant in the lease against sub-letting is within the section, where the breach has not been waived.[22] Clearly such a sub-tenant should be protected as against the tenant. There is no direct authority, but it was held in *Bolton Building Society* v. *Cobb*[23] that the provision did not protect a tenant against the landlord's mortgagee in cases where the tenancy was not binding on the mortgagee.

These provisions apply also where the right to recover possession arises on the death of a statutory tenant within the Rent Act, there being no statutory tenant by succession.[24]

---

[18] R.A. 1977, ss.2, 98; *post*, p. 69.
[19] Defined in s.81(1) as meaning a protected tenancy under R.A. 1977 or within L.T.A. 1954 (Part I or Part II), A.H.A. 1948 or the Rent (Agriculture) Act 1976.
[20] s.8(2). As to licensees generally, s.6 of the Criminal Law Act 1977 should be considered.
[21] Housing Act 1980, s.69, applying to such licences entered into after the commencement of s.69.
[22] For the view that such a sub-tenant is not within the section see Farrand and Arden, *Rent Acts and Regulations* (2nd ed.), p. 229.
[23] [1966] 1 W.L.R. 1.
[24] s.3(3).

Finally, section 4 of the Act makes special provision for agricultural employees, and section 5 provides that, in the case of a residential letting, a notice to quit (by either party) must be at least four weeks, in writing, and contain certain prescribed information.

Contracting Out of the Rent Act

Although the Rent Act contains no express prohibition on contracting out,[25] it has long been accepted by the courts that it is not possible for the parties to contract out of the statutory protection.[26] A recent example is *Street* v. *Mountford*,[27] where a written agreement purported to create a licence, and stated that the occupier understood and accepted that "a licence in the above form does not and is not intended to give me a tenancy protected under the Rent Acts." This term did not prevent the House of Lords from finding a Rent Act tenancy.

This leads on to the following point: while the parties cannot contract out of the the Rent Act, they can so arrange their affairs that the Rent Act does not apply, provided the transaction is not a sham.[28] So, for example, the Rent Act can be avoided, as we will see, by the creation of a holiday letting, or by the provision of board, or, subject to what is said below, by the creation of a licence instead of a tenancy.

The difficulty lies in determining whether a transaction is to be regarded as a sham, and hence as evasion rather than avoidance of the Act.

Differing attitudes have been displayed by the courts in recent years. The Court of Appeal in *Somma* v. *Hazelhurst*,[29] in upholding a "sharing licence" as an effective mechanism to avoid the Rent Act, said,

> "We can see no reason why an ordinary landlord . . . should not be able to grant a licence to occupy an ordinary house if that is what both he and the licensee intend and if they can

---

[25] *Cf.* A.H.A. 1948, s.3(4); Agricultural Holdings (Notices to Quit) Act 1977, s.1(1); L.T.A. 1954, s.38(1); L.R.A. 1967, s.23(1).

[26] *Baxter* v. *Eckersley* [1950] 1 K.B. 480 at 485; *Brown* v. *Draper* [1944] K.B. 309 at 313. See also *R.* v. *Bloomsbury and Marylebone County Court, ex p. Blackburne* (1985) 275 E.G. 1273.

[27] [1985] A.C. 809.

[28] *Foster* v. *Robinson* [1951] 1 K.B. 149 at 158.

[29] [1978] 1 W.L.R. 1014 at 1024–1025. See also *Aldrington Garages* v. *Fielder* (1978) 274 E.G. 557 at 559.

frame any written agreement in such a way as to demonstrate
that it is not really an agreement for a lease masquerading as a
licence, we can see no reason in law or justice why they should
be prevented from achieving that object. Nor can we see why
their common intentions should be categorised as bogus or
unreal or as sham merely on the ground that the court dis-
approves of the bargain."

This may be contrasted with the view of the Court of Appeal in
Buchmann v. *May*,[30] concerning a holiday letting, that "in a context such as the present the court would be astute to detect a sham
where it appears that a provision has been inserted for the purpose
of depriving a tenant of statutory protection under the Rent Acts"
(adding, however, that the burden of proof was upon the tenant to
establish that the provision was a sham).

It is likely that, as a result of *Street* v. *Mountford*,[31] discussed
below, the courts will show an increasing readiness to categorise a
scheme intended to deny statutory protection as a sham. As a
background to this decision a few points should be made about
licences. Unless the occupier has a tenancy, he cannot receive the
full protection of the Act, which requires the property to be *let* as a
separate dwellings.[32] However, a licensee who enjoys exclusive
possession can fall within the definition of a restricted contract[33]
and hence get the benefit of rent control and the requirement of a
court order for possession.[34] A licence cannot be a restricted contract unless the occupier enjoys exclusive occupation of at least
part of a house.[35]

Thus a licensee not enjoying exclusive occupation would have
no rights at all under the Act. This end could be achieved by a
scheme, upheld by the Court of Appeal in *Somma* v. *Hazelhurst*,[36]
whereby two or more occupiers would sign separate documents,
make separate payments and agree to occupy subject to the rights

---

[30] [1978] 2 All E.R. 993 at 998–999. See also *O'Malley* v. *Seymour* (1978)
250 E.G. 1083 at 1088. In *Samrose Properties* v. *Gibbard* [1958] 1
W.L.R. 235 the Rent Act applied to a short letting at a "premium" and
a low rent, as the premium was in substance rent.
[31] [1985] A.C. 809.
[32] R.A. 1977, s.1.
[33] *Ibid.* s.19(2).
[34] Protection from Eviction Act 1977, s.3., as amended by H.A. 1980,
s.69.
[35] R.A. 1977, s.19(6).
[36] [1978] 1 W.L.R. 1014; *Aldrington Garages* v. *Fielder* (1978) 274 E.G.
557; *Sturolson & Co.* v. *Weniz* (1984) 272 E.G. 326; *cf. O'Malley* v.
Seymour (1978) 250 E.G. 1083; *Demuren* v. *Seal Estates Ltd.* (1978)
249 E.G. 440; *Walsh* v. *Griffiths-Jones* [1978] 2 All E.R. 1002.

of each other (and, sometimes, of third parties) to share the accommodation. These "sharing licences," it was held, prevented any degree of exclusive possession or occupation, and hence fell outside even the restricted contract code. Even without a sharing term, an occupier might be held to be a mere licensee even if he had exclusive possession.[37]

The matter arose before the House of Lords in *Street* v. *Mountford*.[38] A document, called a "licence," gave the right to occupy a furnished room for a weekly sum, the occupier having exclusive possession. This was held to create a tenancy within the Rent Act. Their Lordships, reversing the Court of Appeal, returned to the traditional view that there is a strong presumption of a tenancy if the occupier has exclusive possession. The three hallmarks of a tenancy are *exclusive possession*, for a fixed or periodic *term*, and at a *rent*. If these factors are present, there will be a tenancy unless there is some special circumstance reducing it to a licence. The Court should be concerned to inquire simply whether the residential occupier is a lodger or a tenant. He is a lodger if the owner provides attendance or services which require him to exercise unrestricted access to the premises (although it is, of course, possible to grant a lease whereby services, such as board, are provided). The label on the document is inconclusive, as the legal consequences of the agreement are determined by the effect of its terms. The decision in *Somma* v. *Hazelhurst*[39] was wrong, as the sharing term was a sham. Lord Templeman, with whose judgment all concurred, said "Although the Rent Act must not be allowed to alter or influence the construction of an agreement, the court should, in my opinion, be astute to detect and frustrate sham devices and artificial transactions whose only object is to disguise the grant of a tenancy and to evade the Rent Acts."[40]

The significance of this decision will be readily appreciated. Of course, not all sharing terms are shams (for example, an occupant of a hostel with fluctuating inhabitants may share a room rather than take a more expensive single room, the owner filling vacan-

---

[37] See the Court of Appeal decision in *Street* v. *Mountford* (1984) 271 E.G. 1261. It had long been clear that exclusive possession was not necessarily inconsistent with a licence.

[38] [1985] A.C. 809; [1985] Conv. 328 (R. Street); (1985) 48 M.L.R. 712 (S. Anderson); (1985) 101 L.Q.R. 467; (1985) 44 C.L.J. 351 (S. Tromans). The decision has since been applied in *Royal Philanthropic Society* v. *County* (1985) 276 E.G. 1068; *Bretherton* v. *Paton, infra*, n.42. For an Australian view, see (1986) Conv. 39 (D. N. Clarke).

[39] *Supra*. The difficulty is whether the payment obligations are converted to joint and several liability.

[40] [1985] A.C. 809 at 825.

cies as they occur). However, where the occupant enjoys exclusive possession, special circumstances must be shown to avoid the finding of a tenancy. The House of Lords in *Street* v. *Mountford* gave some guidance as to what amounted to special circumstances. A licence will result if the occupation is due to the owner's generosity[41]; or is referable to another legal relationship[42]; or in the case of a service occupier (living in his employer's property in order to facilitate the performance of his duties rather than for his own convenience). Finally, lack of monetary rent, while not conclusive, is strongly indicative of a licence.[43]

Thus it will be more difficult in future to create an effective licence and thereby avoid the Rent Act.

Terminology

A protected tenancy (defined by section 1[44] of the 1977 Act) is one which, on termination, will become a statutory tenancy, provided the tenant satisfies the requirements of section 2. In other words, it is a tenancy existing under the general law either as a legal estate or an equitable interest. It is sometimes referred to as a contractual tenancy.

A statutory tenancy, on the other hand, arises on termination (by any method) of the protected tenancy, provided the tenant occupies the dwelling-house as his residence.[45] It is not a proprietary interest in the accepted sense, but a personal right conferred by statute.[46]

A distinction was formerly made between two types of tenancy, controlled and regulated. The distinction lay primarily in the fact that the rules as to rent control and the grounds for possession differed. Controlled tenancies, however, were abolished by the Housing Act 1980, section 64. Those which were purely residential were converted to regulated tenancies, while those with a partial business use were converted to tenancies protected by the Landlord and Tenant Act 1954, Part II. Thus the only kind of tenancy receiving the full protection of the Rent Act today is the regulated tenancy. This may be contrasted with tenancies (and certain

---

[41] *Marcroft Wagons Ltd.* v. *Smith* [1951] 2 K.B. 496; *Heslop* v. *Burns* [1974] 1 W.L.R. 1241. (No intent to create legal relations).
[42] *e.g.* a mortgage or a contract for sale. *Cf. Bretherton* v. *Paton, The Times,* March 14, 1986 (intending purchaser's occupation held a tenancy where no sale agreed).
[43] *Barnes* v. *Barratt* [1970] 2 Q.B. 657.
[44] *Post,* p. 13.
[45] R.A. 1977, s.2; *post,* p. 53.
[46] *Post,* p. 53.

licences) receiving the limited protection of the "restricted con-tract" code,[47] whereby the rent is controlled, but there is no secur-ity of tenure as such.

[47] *Post*, p. 106.

Chapter 2

THE PROTECTED TENANCY

There are two basic conditions to be satisfied if a tenancy is to qualify as a protected tenancy. First, by section 1 of the Rent Act 1977, it must be "a tenancy under which a dwelling-house (which may be a house or part of a house) is let as a separate dwelling." Secondly, it must not fall within any of the express exclusions from protection contained in Part I of the Act.[1] These matters will be considered in turn.

The Definition in Section 1

Almost every word of this section has been the subject of litigation. It will be convenient to consider in order the main ingredients of the definition.

(a) "Tenancy"

The only statutory definition of "tenancy" in the Act is simply to the effect that a sub-tenancy is included.[2] It appears, however, that any kind of tenancy is included, whether fixed or periodic, expressly granted or arising by implication. Even a tenancy by estoppel is within the Act, as far as the parties to the estoppel are concerned.[3] No distinction is drawn between properly granted legal tenancies and others. A mere contract for a lease, assuming it to be specifically enforceable, would confer the benefit of the Act on the tenant under the *Walsh* v. *Lonsdale*[4] principle.

More significant is the point that a licence cannot come within section 1, although it can in certain circumstances qualify for the more limited protection of the restricted contract code.[5]

Authorities on the question of whether an agreement creates a tenancy or a licence must now be read in the light of *Street* v. *Mountford*,[6] which was discussed in Chapter 1.[7]

---

[1] The exceptions are found primarily in ss.4–16A.
[2] R.A. 1977, s.152(1). For the position as between sub-tenant and head landlord, see s.137, *post*, Chap. 9.
[3] *Stratford* v. *Syrett* [1958] 1 Q.B. 107.
[4] (1882) 21 Ch.D. 9.
[5] *Post*, Chap. 8.
[6] [1985] A.C. 809.
[7] *Ante*, p. 10.

(b) "House"

Section 1 requires a tenancy of a dwelling-house, which may be a house or part of a house. There is no statutory definition of "house,"[8] but it clearly includes a flat or even a single room.[9]

Questions may arise as to impermanent structures, such as caravans[10] or houseboats.[11] This was recently discussed in *R* v. *Rent Officer of Nottingham Registration Area, ex p. Allen.*[12] Whether a caravan can be a "house" depends on the circumstances of the letting. It would not be a "house" if let as a moveable chattel, but would be more likely to qualify if completely immobile. There would be difficult borderline cases, but the Rent Officer should be on guard where the landlord rented out caravans long term, but made superficial arrangements to show some mobility in order to avoid the Act. In the present case, movement from time to time and the ease of disconnection of services (*e.g.* water, electricity, sewage) meant that the caravan was not a "house." It was added that the landlord should act before registration of the rent (on the basis of a protected tenancy) rather than seek judicial review later in the High Court.[13]

A different point on the meaning of "house" is that two distinct properties, let together as one home, can qualify as a "house," for example two flats.[14] This is relevant also to the meaning of the words "a separate dwelling," and is discussed below.

(c) "Let"

The meaning of "tenancy" has already been discussed, and nothing further need be added here.

(d) "As"

The dwelling-house must be let *as* a separate dwelling; in other words, residence must be contemplated by the lease. If the lease is

---

[8] *Cf.* Leasehold Reform Act 1967, s.2, giving a narrow (and much litigated) definition because there the property must be such that, on enfranchisement, it can exist as a separate freehold.

[9] See *Curl* v. *Angelo* [1948] 2 All E.R. 189; *cf. Metropolitan Properties Co.* v. *Barder* [1968] 1 W.L.R. 286.

[10] See also Caravan Sites Act 1968; Mobile Homes Act 1983 (substantially repealing the Act of 1975).

[11] For further examples, see Woodfall, *Landlord and Tenant* (28th ed.), para. 3030; Megarry's *Rent Acts* (10th ed.), p. 50; Halsbury (4th ed.), Vol. 27, para. 583.

[12] (1985) 275 E.G. 251; [1985] Conv. 353 (J.E.M.).

[13] The county court can declare the status of the tenancy, but cannot expunge the registration.

[14] *Langford Property Co.* v. *Goldrich* [1949] 1 K.B. 511.

silent on the matter, then the nature of the premises must be considered. If that also fails to reveal the purpose of the letting, then the *de facto* user is looked at as a last resort.

In *Ponder* v. *Hillman*[15] the lease described the property as "all that shop and premises." The fact that the property was being used as dwelling accommodation at the date of the proceedings did not bring it within the Rent Act, as residence was not contemplated by the lease. *A fortiori* if the lease actually prohibits residential user.[16] However, even though not initially let as a dwelling, the property may subsequently be so treated if the landlord has affirmatively assented to a change of user. Mere knowledge does not suffice.[17]

Difficult questions can arise where property is initially let for more than one purpose.[18] In *Pulleng* v. *Curran*[19] property was let for both business and residential purposes, but the tenant claimed that the business user had ceased. It was held that it had not, but even if it had, it did not follow that the Rent Act now applied. The property was not let as a dwelling, but as a mixed entity. Similarly in *Russell* v. *Booker*,[20] where a mixed residential and agricultural letting was initially protected as an agricultural holding. The agricultural use declined, so that the tenancy ceased to be an agricultural holding, but this did not bring it within the Rent Act. A unilateral change of user by the tenant would not suffice. Here the tenant could only succeed if there was a subsequent contract, or if the landlord had accepted rent for many years with full actual knowledge of the change of user.

It may be helpful to summarise briefly the various possible permutations. First, the question may arise as to the intitial status of the letting. If it is let for a single purpose, then, as we have seen, the Rent Act can only apply if that purpose is residential.[21] If it is initially let for a dual purpose, then the Rent Act is unlikely to

---

[15] [1969] 1 W.L.R. 1261.

[16] See *Cooper* v. *Henderson* (1982) 263 E.G. 592, where the prohibition had been openly broken for some years. As the breach was continuing, waiver was not established. The prohibition, it was said, was not a sham to evade the Rent Act.

[17] *Wolfe* v. *Hogan* [1949] 2 K.B. 194.

[18] See generally [1983] Conv. 390 (J. Martin).

[19] (1982) 44 P. & C.R. 58. The initial letting could not be within the Rent Act. See L.T.A. 1954, s.23(1); R.A. 1977, s.24(3).

[20] (1982) 263 E.G. 513.

[21] *cf.* the business and agricultural codes, where there is no requirement that the property be initially let for those specific purposes. See L.T.A. 1954, s.23(1); A.H.A. 1948, s.1, as amended by A.H.A. 1984, Sched. 3.

apply. In the case of a mixed business and residential letting, the Landlord and Tenant Act 1954, Part II, will apply unless the business element is minimal.[22] If the letting is part residential and part agricultural, then the Agricultural Holdings Act 1948 will apply if the agricultural user is predominant.[23]

Secondly, the question may arise on a subsequent change of user. If the letting changes from solely business (or agricultural) to solely residential, then the Rent Act cannot apply unless a new contract can be inferred.[24] Similarly if the letting is initially for mixed business (or agricultural) and residential purposes, and the business (or agricultural) user ceases.[25] Finally, the letting may change from an initial sole use to a mixed use. If a residential letting acquires a business element, the 1954 Act will apply unless the business element is minimal.[26] The 1954 Act will also apply where a business letting takes on a residential element.[27] If a residential letting takes on an agricultural element, the Rent Act will continue to apply until the agricultural use becomes predominant and thereby takes the tenancy into the Agricultural Holdings Act.[28] In the converse case, where an agricultural holding takes on a residential element, the Agricultural Holdings Act continues to apply unless the residential aspect becomes dominant, in which case there is no protection at all.[29]

(e) "A"

The house must be let as *a* separate dwelling, meaning one dwelling and not two or more. So in *Horford Investments* v. *Lambert*[30] the letting of a house already converted to multiple dwelling units was not a protected tenancy. Perhaps a more borderline case

---

[22] *Post*, p. 32.
[23] *Russell* v. *Booker*, *supra*; A.H.A. 1948, s.1, as amended by A.H.A. 1984, Sched. 3; R.A. 1977, s.26.
[24] *Wolfe* v. *Hogan*, *supra*.
[25] *Pulleng* v. *Curran*, *supra*; *Russell* v. *Booker*, *supra*.
[26] *Lewis* v. *Weldcrest Ltd* [1978] 1 W.L.R. 1107, *post*, p. 32.
[27] *Ponder* v. *Hillman*, *supra*.
[28] R.A. 1977, s.10; A.H.A. 1948, s.1, as amended by A.H.A. 1984, Sched. 3.
[29] By analogy with *Russell* v. *Booker*, *supra*.
[30] [1976] Ch. 39. Such a tenancy could be within L.T.A. 1954, Part II, if there is a sufficient degree of occupation by the tenant; *Lee-Verhulst (Investments) Ltd.* v. *Harwood Trust* [1972] 1 Q.B. 204; *cf. Bagettes Ltd.* v. *G. P. Estates Co. Ltd* [1956] Ch. 290. A subsequent conversion would not cause the tenancy to be outside s.1; *Carter* v. *S.U. Carburettor Co.* [1942] 2 K.B. 288.

is *St. Catherine's College* v. *Dorling*,[31] where a house was let to the college for sub-letting to students. The house contained rooms suitable for use as study/bedsitting rooms by five students who would share the kitchen and bathroom, but it had not been converted to multiple units. The college sought a rent reduction on the basis that the tenancy was protected, but it was held that the Rent Act did not apply. The property was not let as *a* dwelling, but as several. In such cases the sub-tenancies may be protected as against the tenant, even though the tenancy is not itself protected.[32]

The point discussed above involves the situation where one property has been let as several dwellings. The converse case is where two or more properties have been let together as one dwelling. In such a case the tenancy may be protected. In *Langford Property Co. Ltd.* v. *Goldrich*[33] two self-contained flats, which were separately rated and not adjoining, but which were used as one home, were held to constitute one dwelling. This may be contrasted with *Metropolitan Properties Co. Ltd.* v. *Barder*[34] where a protected tenant of a flat was later granted a tenancy of a room across the corridor. The rent was paid by the same cheque. When the landlord gave notice to quit the room, the tenant claimed protection for the room and the flat together. He failed, as the Act could only apply if the room was let with the flat as a single unit, whereas here it was let by a different contract and on different terms. Nor, on the facts, was the room a separate dwelling on its own.

Finally, in *Grosvenor (Mayfair) Estates* v. *Amberton*[35] two flats were let by the same demise. At that time one was occupied by licensees, with only a remote possibility that the two could be occupied together. There was, however, a covenant to use them as a "strictly private residence." It was held that the covenant did not displace the evidence that they were not let as a separate dwelling. It might have been otherwise if the parties had contemplated the early removal of the licensees and the idea that the tenant would then live in both. In other words, it was not fatal to the argument

---

[31] [1980] 1 W.L.R. 66. For the possible application of L.T.A. 1954, Part II in such a case, see *Groveside Properties Ltd.* v. *Westminster Medical School* (1983) 47 P. & C.R. 507, *post*, p. 27.

[32] Unless the sub-tenancy is a student letting or otherwise excluded. For protection against the head landlord, see R.A. s.137(3), *post*, p. 128.

[33] [1949] 1 K.B. 511. For similar problems arising under s.2, see *Kavanagh* v. *Lyroudias* [1985] 1 All E.R. 560.

[34] [1968] 1 W.L.R. 286.

[35] (1985) 265 E.G. 693.

that the tenant could not get immediate possession of both flats. Here, however, they were let as two flats, subject to the future possibility of their use as one dwelling at an unspecified date. This did not suffice.

(f) "Separate"

The question whether a dwelling is "separate" depends primarily on the extent to which any accommodation is shared, and with whom. The occupant must enjoy exclusive possession of some accommodation before there can be a tenancy at all. In addition to the demised premises, however, the tenant may be entitled to share certain rooms, such as a kitchen or bathroom, either with his landlord or with other tenants. These two situations will be considered in turn. It should be noted that the question of sharing under discussion here is sharing under the terms of the tenancy.[36]

As far as sharing with the landlord is concerned, a distinction grew up between "living accommodation" and other accommodation. If the tenant shared "living accommodation" with his landlord, then he was not fully protected, but had the benefit of what is now a restricted contract. If, however, the shared accommodation was not "living accommodation," then the tenant was fully protected. What, then, is meant by "living accommodation"? The basic test is that rooms where simultaneous use is likely are "living" rooms. Thus kitchens[37] and sitting rooms are within the description, while, generally speaking, bathrooms[38] and halls are not. Much depends, however, on the extent of the shared user in the particular case.[39] The rationale of this rule is clear: it would be undesirable to confer security of tenure in such cases of sharing, which involve "the right of simultaneous use of a living room in such a manner that the privacy of the landlord or tenant, as the case may be, is invaded."[40] The present rules are contained in section 21 of the 1977 Act, providing that the tenant has a restricted contract in cases where the sharing precludes a protected tenancy.

Much of the old learning on shared accommodation has been made redundant by the introduction of the resident landlord rules by the 1974 Act. These rules, as we will see,[41] operate to give the tenant a restricted contract instead of a protected tenancy. The resident landlord rules do not require any element of sharing, but

---

[36] R.A. 1977, ss.21–23.
[37] *Neale* v. *Del Soto* [1945] K.B. 144.
[38] *Goodrich* v. *Paisner* [1957] A.C. 65.
[39] *Ibid*; *Marsh Ltd.* v. *Cooper* [1969] 1 W.L.R. 803.
[40] *Goodrich* v. *Paisner, supra*, at p. 76.
[41] *Post*, Chap. 3.

merely that the landlord should be resident in the same building. In the case of sharing, discussed above, there will be a resident landlord. But the old sharing rules remain significant in the context of tenancies granted before the Act of 1974. In such cases the resident landlord rules do not apply retrospectively, provided the tenancy is unfurnished.[42] So in the case of a pre-1974 unfurnished tenancy granted by a resident landlord, the sharing rules must still be considered.

It remains to consider the position where the tenant, in addition to his separate accommodation, shares other accommodation with persons other than the landlord, for example with other tenants. This situation is dealt with by section 22 of the 1977 Act, providing that the tenant has a protected tenancy of his "separate accommodation" in spite of the sharing element. No distinction is drawn between "living" and other accommodation. Thus a tenancy can be protected even though the tenant has the right to share a kitchen or bathroom with other tenants. In addition to protection for his "separate accommodation," section 22 also protects the tenant in the use of the shared accommodation. Any term in his tenancy providing for the termination or modification of his right to use any of the shared accommodation which is "living accommodation" is of no effect,[43] save to the extent that it permits a variation in the persons in common with whom the tenant can use the shared accommodation, or an increase in their number.[44] No order for possession of the shared accommodation can be made unless a similar order is being (or has been) made as to the separate accommodation.[45] However, that is without prejudice to the power of the county court, on the landlord's application, to make such order as the court thinks just to terminate the tenant's right to use any of the shared accommodation by varying or increasing the number of persons entitled to use it.[46]

(g) "Dwelling"

There is no requirement that the property should be the tenant's own dwelling[47] (although, if it is not, he will not

---

[42] R.A. 1977, Sched. 24, para. 6; *post*, p. 42.
[43] *Ibid*. s.22(3).
[44] *Ibid*. s.22(4).
[45] *Ibid*. s.22(5).
[46] *Ibid*. s.22(6). Such an order can be made only where the terms of the tenancy would permit the termination or modification of the tenant's rights; s.22(7).
[47] *Feather Supplies Ltd.* v. *Ingham* [1971] 2 Q.B. 348 (where father took tenancy for the occupation of his son). See also the cases on company and institutional tenants, *post*, p. 55.

acquire a statutory tenancy[48]). Nor need it to be his sole dwelling.[49]

The test is whether the major activities of daily living, such as sleeping, eating and cooking, are to take place on the premises. In *Wright* v. *Howell*[50] there was a letting of an unfurnished room with no cooking facilities or water supply. The tenant did not sleep on the premises. The Court of Appeal held the tenancy to be unprotected, emphasising the importance of the fact that the tenant slept elsewhere.

But the mere fact of sleeping on the premises is insufficient. In *Curl* v. *Angelo*[51] a hotel-keeper rented two rooms of a house as sleeping accommodation for guests and employees. This was not protected, as a "dwelling" requires more than one residential activity.

Before leaving the definition of a protected tenancy, the contents of section 26 of the 1977 Act should be noted. Section 26 provides that any land or premises let together with a dwelling-house shall, unless it consists of agricultural land exceeding two acres, be treated as part of the dwelling-house. The circumstances here envisaged are that the dwelling is the main part of the letting, the other land or premises being ancillary.[52] The effect of this provision is basically threefold. First, if the tenant has security as to his house, his security extends to property let with it, such as garages, gardens or outhouses.[53] Secondly, when considering the rateable value limits,[54] the entire property must be brought into account and not just the house. Thirdly, neglect of the ancillary property can be the basis of a ground for possession in the same manner as neglect of the house.[55] Finally, the relevant time for considering whether the property is ancillary to the house (or vice versa) is the date of the application to court (or, possibly, the hearing) as opposed to the date of the letting.[56]

---

[48] *Post*, p. 55.
[49] *Langford Property Co. Ltd.* v. *Tureman* [1949] 1 K.B.29.
[50] (1948) 92 S.J. 26.
[51] [1948] 2 All E.R. 189. See also *Lyons* v. *Caffery* (1983) 266 E.G. 213 *post*, p. 37.
[52] Contrast s.6, *post*, p. 24, as to dwelling-houses let together with other land.
[53] *Langford Property Co. Ltd.* v. *Batten* [1951] A.C. 233; *Bradshaw* v. *Smith* (1980) 255 E.G. 699.
[54] *Post*, p. 21.
[55] *Holloway* v. *Povey* (1984) 271 E.G. 195 (neglect of the garden). See Case 3, *post*, p. 76.
[56] *Russell* v. *Booker* (1982) 263 E.G 513.

Tenancies Excluded from Protection

Assuming that the tenancy qualifies under section 1 as the letting of a house as a separate dwelling, it may nevertheless be excluded from protection by the express exceptions primarily contained in sections 4 to 16A of the 1977 Act. Some of the exceptions (such as high rateable value lettings) are based on the nature of the property. Others (such as lettings with board or at a low rent) depend on the terms of the tenancy. Or the exclusion may depend on the status of the landlord (for example Crown or local authority lettings) or of the tenant (as with student lettings). Some of the excluded tenancies will be protected by other statutory codes. It is proposed to deal with them in the order of the Act.

(a) Tenancies above the rateable value limits

The tenancy will be excluded if the demised property exceeded the rateable value limits on the "appropriate day." By section 25(3), the "appropriate day" is March 23, 1965 if the property was then rated, or in any other case (*i.e.* where the property was built after that date) the date it first appeared in the valuation list. Where the demised property is only part of a house, the rateable value of that part alone is considered. In such a case the rateable value of the house must be apportioned.[57] Of course, the rateable value of a property is frequently considerably lower than the amount of rates actually payable. The latter is fixed annually, and is not relevant.

In the following statement of the rateable value limits, the higher figure in each pair relates to Greater London.[58] The limits are set out in section 4, and are as follows:

(a) if the appropriate day is on or after April 1, 1973[59] the limit is £1,500 or £750;

(b) if the appropriate day is on or after March 22, 1973[60] but before April 1, 1973, the tenancy is excluded if the rateable value exceeded £600 or £300 on the appropriate day *and* exceeded £1,500 or £750 on April 1, 1973;

(c) if the appropriate day is before March 22, 1973, the tenancy

---

[57] R.A. 1977, s.25(1).
[58] *Ibid.* s.4(2).
[59] The date the new rating assessments under s.68 of the General Rate Act 1967 took effect.
[60] The date the Counter-Inflation Act 1973 was passed.

is excluded if the rateable value exceeded £400 or £200 on the appropriate day *and* exceeded £600 or £300 on March 22, 1973 *and* exceeded £1,500 or £750 on April 1, 1973.

The complexity of these rules results primarily from the rating revaluation which took place in 1973. A dwelling-house is deemed to be within the rateable value limits unless the contrary is shown.[61] Where the valuation list is altered after the appropriate day with effect from a date not later than the appropriate day, then the value as altered is taken.[62] The effect of this can be seen in *Rodwell* v. *Gwynne Trusts*,[63] where a rateable value of £430 was reduced to £388 (the limit being £400) as from April 1, 1965. As the rateable value on the appropriate day (March 23, 1965) remained £430, the tenancy was not protected, even though a refund was paid which was back-dated to 1963.

These rateable value limits are fairly high. It is unusual for a tenancy to be excluded on this ground. The rationale of the exception is clear: tenants of expensive properties do not need the protection of the Rent Act.

(b) Tenancies at a low rent
By section 5, a tenancy is not protected if it is either rent-free, or if the rent is less than two-thirds of the rateable value on the appropriate day (as defined above).

The main purpose of this provision is to exclude long leases from the Rent Act. Long leaseholders normally pay a premium and, thereafter, a ground rent, which will usually be less than two-thirds of the rateable value on the appropriate day. Such tenancies do not need the protection of the Rent Act, because they are protected by the similar provisions of Part I of the Landlord and Tenant Act 1954 (and sometimes by the Leasehold Reform Act 1967). However, there is no exclusion of long leases as such from the Rent Act. If the rent exceeds the two-thirds figure, the tenancy will, therefore, be protected.

While the rateable value is fixed at the appropriate day, the rent level is determined when the matter arises. In other words it is the current rent which must be at least two-thirds of the fixed rateable value figure. Thus a tenancy can fall out of protection if a rent

---

[61] R.A. 1977, s.4(3); *R.* v. *Westminster (City) London Borough Rent Officer, ex p. Rendall* [1973] 1 Q.B. 859. Disputes go to the county court; *ibid.* s.25(2).
[62] *Ibid.* s.25(4).
[63] [1970] 1 W.L.R. 327.

reduction takes it below the two-thirds figure.[64] Similarly, a rent increase can bring the tenancy into protection.

What is meant by "rent" for the purpose of section 5? If no monetary rent is paid, services can constitute rent at common law, but can only be rent for Rent Act purposes if quantifiable. So if a tenant who is an employee of the landlord pays no rent but is paid a smaller wage on that account, his tenancy can be protected, the rent being the amount by which his wages have been reduced.[65]

Another point is that "rent," for the purpose of section 5, means the total money payment payable by the tenant to the landlord.[66] In the case of long tenancies (exceeding 21 years), however, section 5(4) provides that "rent" does not include any sums payable by the tenant which are expressed to be payable in respect of rates, services, repairs, maintenance or insurance. The purpose of this provision is to prevent a long tenancy being brought into the Rent Act by an increase in the service charge.[67]

A premium, if genuine, is not "rent," but a sum described as a premium may be treated as rent if it is a sham device to evade the Rent Act, as is likely to be the case where a premium is payable on the grant of a short lease. In *Samrose Properties* v. *Gibbard*[68] a short lease was granted at a "premium" and a nominal rent. It was held that the "premium" was in fact rent, so that the tenancy was protected.

Finally, special rules apply to controlled tenancies, upon their conversion to regulated tenancies, so that they are not prejudiced by the fact that the rent may have been less than two-thirds of the rateable value.[69]

---

[64] The position may be otherwise in the case of a statutory tenancy. See also *Williams* v. *Khan* (1982) 43 P. & C.R. 1, noted at [1980] Conv. 389–392 and [1981] Conv. 325–326, where the view is taken that rent "payable" under s.5 means the contractual rent, so that a reduction in the registered rent by the Rent Officer would not cause the protection to cease.

[65] *Montagu* v. *Browning* [1954] 1 W.L.R. 1039; *cf. Barnes* v. *Barratt* [1970] 2 Q.B. 657, where the services were unquantifiable. See also Farrand and Arden, *Rent Acts and Regulations* (2nd ed.), p. 9, suggesting a loop-hole of a rent-free letting with a charge for the hire of the furniture. It is considered, however, that this would be regarded as a sham. See also R.A. 1977, s.71(1), *post*, p. 139.

[66] *Sidney Trading Co. Ltd.* v. *Finsbury Borough Council* [1952] 1 All E.R. 460, at 461.

[67] This would result in the tenant being unable to charge a premium on assignment, subject to R.A. 1977, s.127, *post*, p. 156.

[68] [1958] 1 W.L.R. 235.

[69] R.A. 1977, Sched. 17, para. 5, as amended by H.A. 1980, Sched. 25, para. 59. See also R.A. 1977, s.5(2), as to tenancies brought into protection by the Counter-Inflation Act 1973, and H.A. 1980, s.73 and Sched. 8, para. 1, as to protected Crown lettings.

(c) Tenancy of a dwelling-house let together with other land

Section 6 provides that, subject to section 26, a tenancy is not protected if the dwelling-house is let together with land other than the site of the dwelling-house. Section 26, as we have seen,[70] provides that land or premises let together with the dwelling-house shall be treated as part of it save in the case of agricultural land exceeding two acres. The distinction between these two provisions lies in the meaning of "let together with." Section 26 refers to other property which is ancillary to the dwelling. Section 6 deals with the converse case, where the dwelling is ancillary to some other property which is the main subject of the letting. Thus in *Feyereisal* v. *Turnidge*[71] the Rent Act did not apply to a letting of a campsite which included a bungalow, because the bungalow was an adjunct to the campsite. The relevant time for deciding what is the dominant purpose of the letting is the date of the application to court (or, possibly, the hearing), and not the start of the tenancy.[72]

A dwelling-house can be "let together with" other property (or vice versa) even though the lettings are not in the same document.[73] Nor need the properties be contiguous.[74] The tenant's position is not changed by the fact that there is a subsequent severance of the reversion, so that there are different landlords of the dwelling and the other property.[75]

It should be added, however, that most of the case law on section 6 deals with mixed lettings of business and residential property. Such lettings could formerly exist as controlled tenancies, but cannot be regulated tenancies. Any element of business user (which is more than *de minimis*) brings the tenancy within Part II of the Landlord and Tenant Act 1954. Such a tenancy cannot, therefore, be protected, irrespective of section 6.

Finally, although the tenancy of a dwelling let together with other property cannot be protected, any subtenancy of the dwelling-house alone can be protected as against the tenant and as against the head landlord.[76]

(d) Tenancies with board or attendance

A tenancy is not protected if the dwelling-house is bona fide let at a rent which includes payments in respect of board or attend-

---

[70] *Ante*, p. 20.
[71] [1952] 2 Q.B. 29.
[72] *Russell* v. *Booker* (1982) 263 E.G. 513.
[73] *Wimbush* v. *Cibulia* [1949] 2 K.B. 564.
[74] *Langford Property Co.* v. *Batten* [1951] A.C. 223 (flat and garage).
[75] *Jelley* v. *Buckman* [1974] Q.B. 488.
[76] R.A. 1977, s.137(3). *Post*, p. 128.

ance.[77] While any payments (which are not *de minimis*) in respect of board exclude the tenancy from protection, payments in respect of attendance do not have this result unless the amount of rent fairly attributable to attendance, having regard to the value of the attendance to the tenant, forms a substantial part of the rent.[78]

A tenancy excluded from protection by section 7 can be a restricted contract unless, in the case of board, the payments form a substantial proportion of the rent.[79] Thus no tenancy with board can be regulated. If the board is less than substantial, it can be a restricted contract. If it is substantial, it is outside the Act altogether. In the case of attendance, however, the tenancy is regulated if the payments for it are less than substantial, otherwise it is a restricted contract. It is never outside the Act altogether. These matters are decided as at the date of the grant of the tenancy.

The rationale of the rule is that it would be unduly onerous if a landlord who was obliged by the terms of the tenancy[80] to provide these services should have to provide them indefinitely to a tenant with security of tenure. However, the lack of definition of "board" and "attendance" has given rise to the possibility of evasion.

As the dwelling must be a bona fide let at a rent including payments for board and attendance, clearly these services must be genuinely provided, otherwise the term is disregarded as a sham.[81] Apart from that, the section contains little guidance.

There is little authority on "board." Clearly it need not be full board, but must be more than *de minimis* (for example, an early morning cup of tea.[82]) "Continental" breakfast has been held sufficient in Scotland.[83] While a cooked meal may not be necessary, it is suggested that the mere provision of groceries (or even the installation of a vending machine) would not constitute board.

---

[77] *Ibid.* s.7(1). See also s.23. Of course, the provision of board and attendance can indicate a licence only, but there is no reason why a tenancy cannot be created with such terms.

[78] *Ibid.* s.7(2).

[79] *Ibid.* s.19(5), *post*, p. 108.

[80] s.7 does not apply if the board or attendance are voluntarily provided.

[81] *Palser* v. *Grinling* [1948] A.C. 291; *Wilkes* v. *Goodwin*, [1923] 2 K.B. 86.

[82] *Wilkes* v. *Goodwin, supra*; *cf. R.* v. *Battersea, Wandsworth, Mitcham and Wimbledon Rent Tribunal, ex p. Parikh*, [1957] 1 W.L.R. 410, suggesting that a sandwich is "board."

[83] *Holiday Flat Co.* v. *Kuczera*, 1978, S.L.T. (Sh. Ct.) 47; *cf.* the county court decision in *Dale (Rita)* v. *Adrahill and Ali Khan* [1982] C.L.Y. 1787 (held no board where breakfast was available in a different building 250 yards away, and not everyone took breakfast).

"Attendance" means the provision of services which are personal to the tenant, such as cleaning his room, supplying clean linen, delivering his mail, or taking away his refuse. It does not embrace services performed for lessees in common, such as cleaning the common parts or providing central heating.[84] In *Marchant* v. *Charters*[85] the occupier of a room in a residential hotel could get a meal from the housekeeper, and was entitled to the provision of clean linen and the cleaning of his room. He was held, in fact, to be a licensee, but even if there had been a tenancy, it would not have been protected because these services constituted substantial attendance.

Many of the authorities on the meaning of "substantial" were decided before the Rent Act 1974, at a time when substantial payments for furniture also took the tenancy out of protection. While this is no longer the case, the decisions on furnished lettings remain useful guides as to the meaning of "substantial" in the context of attendance. A broad, non-arithmetical approach is the correct one.[86] The matter is further discussed in Chapter 3.[87]

(e) Student lettings

Section 8, re-enacting a provision introduced by the 1974 Act, excludes from protection a tenancy granted to a person "who is pursuing, or intends to pursue, a course of study[88] provided by a specified[89] educational institution." The tenancy must be granted by that institution or by another specified institution or body of persons. The time for determining the applicability of section 8 is the grant of the tenancy.

The purpose of the exception is to prevent security of tenure of college accommodation arising in favour of former students, to the detriment of the current student population. Such lettings may, however, fall within the restricted contract code, from which they are not expressly excluded.

Another result of section 8 is that where the property is subject to such student lettings during part of the year, the institution can

---

[84] *Palser* v. *Grinling, supra.*

[85] [1977] 1 W.L.R. 1181.

[86] *Palser* v. *Grinling, supra*; *Woodward* v. *Docherty* [1974] 1 W.L.R. 966.

[87] *Post*, p. 43.

[88] It is not clear whether taking a sabbatical year, for example to carry out Students' Union activities, would be included.

[89] By statutory instrument; s.8(2). See the Protected Tenancies (Exceptions) Regulations, 1974 (S.I. 1974/1366), as amended, and 1976 (S.I. 1976/905).

let the property at other times, *i.e.* during the vacation, with the benefit of a mandatory ground to recover possession on termination of the vacation letting.[90]

The specified institutions include universities, colleges, polytechnics and certain institutions for higher education. Private landlords are not within this section, as they are not within the policy of the exception, although it might be argued that the student accommodation shortage would be eased if private lettings were similarly treated. However, a private landlord can indirectly obtain the benefit of the section by letting to the educational institution with a covenant against sub-letting except on excluded student lettings. The letting to the institution may be protected tenancy, and therefore subject to rent control, but cannot become a statutory tenancy on termination, because an institution cannot "reside."[91] On termination of the head lease, the student sub-tenants will have no security against the head landlord.[92] Such a scheme is illustrated by *St. Catherine's College* v. *Dorling*,[93] where, however, even the head tenancy was unprotected because, on the facts, the house was not let "as a separate dwelling." Such schemes are not frowned upon as evasion devices, but rather encouraged as easing the student accommodation shortage.[94]

The implications in the decision in *Groveside Properties Ltd.* v. *Westminster Medical School*[95] for these private landlord schemes should, however, be noted. In that case a furnished flat was let to the School to house its students. The School paid the outgoings and kept keys, and the Secretary of the School made frequent visits. The School's tenancy was held to be a business tenancy within Part II of the Landlord and Tenant Act 1954. The School had a sufficient degree of occupation, and the running of the medical school was within the statutory definition of "business" which, by section 23(2), includes any "activity" by a body of persons. While, of course, the medical school was not run on the demised premises, the fostering of a collegiate spirit was carried on there, and this was part of the educational process. So the landlord avoided the Rent Act, but found himself subject to the 1954 Act, under which the tenant, while having to pay the market rent, has

---

[90] R.A. 1977, Sched. 15, Case 14, *post*, p. 87.
[91] *Post*, p. 55.
[92] See R.A. 1977, s.137, *post*, p. 120. Sub-tenants who are not protected as against the tenant are not within s.137.
[93] [1980] 1 W.L.R. 66, *ante*, p. 17.
[94] *Ibid.*
[95] (1983) 47 P. & C.R. 507; [1984] Conv. 57 (J.E.M.).

security of tenure. Of course it is not argued that all institutional
student lettings will qualify as business tenancies as a result of this
case, but the landlord should be aware of the possible application
of the 1954 Act.

Finally, it might be added that the occupation of a college Hall
of Residence is not likely to be a protected tenancy even apart
from section 8. First, it is more likely to be a licence than a
tenancy, and secondly, even if a tenancy, it is likely to be excluded
by section 7 (board and attendance).

(f) Holiday lettings

Like student lettings, this exception was first introduced by the
1974 Act. The current provision is section 9 of the 1977 Act,
whereby a tenancy is not protected "if the purpose of the tenancy
is to confer on the tenant the right to occupy the dwelling-house
for a holiday." Such lettings are also excluded from the restricted
contract code.[96]

As in the case of student lettings, where the property is subject
to a holiday letting for part of the year, the landlord can let the
property at other times, *i.e.* out of season, with the benefit of a
mandatory ground to recover possession on termination of the out
of season letting.[97]

The lack of a statutory definition of "holiday" has encouraged
attempts at evasion by landlords. Of course, most cases of holiday
occupation do not involve tenancies. Even if they do, it might be
argued that the property is not let as a *dwelling*. However that may
be, the problem is to know what is meant by a holiday letting. The
leading case is *Buchmann* v. *May*,[98] involving a three-month letting to a New Zealand national with a temporary visitor's permit.
She had already occupied for about two years under a series of
short lettings. The document, signed by the tenant, stated that the
letting was "solely for the purpose of the tenant's holiday in the
London area." The Court of Appeal took the dictionary meaning
of "holiday" as "a period of cessation from work or a period of
recreation" as a workable definition, if not too narrowly construed. It was held that where the tenancy is stated to be for a holiday, the onus is upon the tenant to establish that the document is a
sham, or the result of a mistake or misrepresentation, adding that
the court would be astute to detect a sham where it appeared that

[96] R.A. 1977, s.19(7).
[97] *Ibid*. Sched. 15, Case 13.
[98] [1978] 2 All E.R. 993.

the term had been inserted to deprive the tenant of Rent Act protection. On the facts, the tenant failed to discharge this onus, so the tenancy was not protected.

The tenants succeeded in *R.* v. *Rent Officer for the London Borough of Camden, ex p. Plant,*[99] involving a letting for six months, where it was held that the landlord could not have genuinely intended a holiday letting when he knew that the tenants would occupy for the purpose of their work as student nurses. The tenant might also succeed if, being a foreigner with language difficulties, he can show that he did not understand the terms of the lease.[1]

It has been held in the county court that the common concept of a "working holiday" is included in the meaning of "holiday."[2] It should be added that disputes as to the status of the tenancy frequently arise upon an attempt to register a "fair rent." The jurisdiction of the Rent Officer in such a case is discussed in Chapter 10.[3]

(g) Agricultural tenancies

A tenancy is not protected if the dwelling is comprised in an agricultural holding[4] and is occupied by the person responsible for the control of the farming of the holding.[5] Such tenancies enjoy security of tenure under the agricultural code. The applicability of this exception is judged as at the date of the application to court.[6] Unlike the Rent Act, the Agricultural Holdings Act does not require that the letting be initially for agricultural purposes. Hence it is possible for a tenancy to move out of Rent Act protection on a subsequent change to agricultural user, but the converse is not possible.[7]

---

[99] (1980) 257 E.G. 713. See also *R.* v. *Rent Officer for Camden, ex p. Ebiri* [1981] 1 W.L.R. 881.

[1] See *Francke* v. *Hakmi* (unreported), discussed in [1984] Conv. 286 (T. J. Lyons).

[2] *McHale* v. *Daneham* (1979) 249 E.G. 969 (6 months letting, extended to 9 months, of property in Maida Vale, to foreign tenants); *cf. R.* v. *Croydon and South West London Rent Tribunal, ex p. Ryzewska* [1977] Q.B. 876. For an examination of various county court and unreported cases, see [1984] Conv. 286 (T. J. Lyons).

[3] *Post*, p. 147. See particularly *R.* v. *Rent Officer for Camden, ex p. Ebiri*, *supra*.

[4] As defined by Agricultural Holdings Act 1948, s.1, as amended by Agricultural Holdings Act 1984, Sched. 3.

[5] R.A. 1977, s.10.

[6] *Russell* v. *Booker* (1982) 263 E.G. 513; [1983] Conv. 390 (J. Martin).

[7] *Russell* v. *Booker*, *supra*, discussed *ante*, p. 15.

If a dwelling which is part of an agricultural holding is sublet, the sub-tenant may be protected against the tenant, and also against the head landlord.[8]

(*h*) *Licensed premises*

By section 11, a tenancy is not protected if the dwelling-house consists or comprises premises licensed for the sale of intoxicating liquors for consumption on the premises. As far as off-licences are concerned, they will be excluded by section 24[9] on the ground that they are business tenancies within Part II of the Landlord and Tenant Act 1954. Section 24 is insufficient to exclude on-licensed premises, because such tenancies are excluded from the business tenancy code by section 43(1) of the 1954 Act. Hence the necessity for section 11 to exclude them. However, it is doubtful whether, in many cases, tenancy of such premises could satisfy the basic requirement of section 1 that it be a tenancy of a house let as a dwelling.[10]

Public-houses, therefore, fall outside the protection of both the residential and business codes.

(*i*) *Tenancies granted by resident landlords*

Such tenancies are excluded from protection by section 12, but are within the restricted contract code. They are fully discussed in Chapter 3.

(*j*) *Crown lettings*

Such lettings were formerly excluded by section 13 of the 1977 Act, but this has been amended by section 73 of the Housing Act 1980. The present position is that a tenancy is excluded where the interest of the immediate landlord belongs to the Crown or to a government department, but can be protected where the interest of the immediate landlord belongs to the Duchies of Lancaster or Cornwall, or is under the management of the Crown Estate Commissioners. The position is similar in respect of restricted contracts. The 1980 amendment applies retrospectively, provided the tenancy was still in existence when it came into effect.[11]

---

[8] R.A. 1977, s.137(3), reversing *Maunsell* v. *Olins* [1975] A.C. 373. See also the Rent (Agriculture) Act 1976.
[9] *Post*, p. 32.
[10] By analogy with *Pulleng* v. *Curran* (1982) 44 P. & C.R. 58, *ante*, p. 15.
[11] *Crown Estate Commissioners* v. *Wordsworth* (1982) 44 P. & C.R. 302. As to the rent, see H.A. 1980, s.73 and Sched. 8, para. 1.

The fact that the head landlord is the Crown does not preclude a protected tenancy in favour of a sub-tenant, as against the tenant.

As the application of section 13 depends on the current ownership of the landlord's interest, as opposed to the circumstances at the grant of the tenancy, a tenancy can become, or cease to be, protected on an assignment of the landlord's interest by or to the Crown, as the case may be.

(k) *Local authority lettings*

Section 14 excludes a tenancy from protection when the interest of the immediate landlord belongs at any time to a local authority (or to various other bodies, such as the Commission for the New Towns). As with Crown lettings, the matter is not judged as at the grant of the tenancy, but depends on the current ownership of the reversion. Hence the tenant's status can be changed by a transfer of the reversion.

Since the Housing Act 1980 (now Part IV of the 1985 Act) it is possible for local authority tenants to have security of tenure under the new concept of the "secure tenancy." Such tenancies are outside the scope of this book.

Tenancies excluded from protection by section 14 are similarly excluded from the restricted contract code.[12]

(l) *Housing association tenancies*

Tenancies are excluded by section 15 at any time when the interest of the immediate landlord belongs to certain housing associations, housing trusts or the Housing Corporation. "Housing association" and "housing trust" are defined by the section.[12a]

Tenancies granted by the above-mentioned bodies are brought within the fair rent system by section 86 of the 1977 Act, provided they would qualify as protected tenancies but for their exclusion by section 15.

Subject to certain conditions, these tenancies are included in the "secure tenancy" scheme by section 80 of the Housing Act 1985.

(m) *Housing co-operative tenancies*

Similarly excluded, by section 16, are tenancies in respect of which the immediate landlord's interest at any time belongs to a housing co-operative, as defined by the Housing Act 1985.

Such tenancies may also qualify as "secure tenancies" under section 80 of the 1985 Act.

---

[12] R.A. 1977, s.19(5), as amended by H.A. 1980.
[12a] As amended by Housing (Consequential Provisions) Act 1985, Sched. 2.

(n) Assured tenancies

Assured tenancies were introduced by the Housing Act 1980. Such tenancies are excluded from the Rent Act.[13] These are residential tenancies granted by "approved bodies" (such as pension funds), in respect of buildings erected after the 1980 Act. There is no rent control, but the tenant has security of tenure modelled upon the business tenancy code. These tenancies are further discussed in Chapter 4.

(o) Tenancies of premises with a business use

Section 24 of the 1977 Act provides that a tenancy cannot be regulated if it is a tenancy to which Part II of the Landlord and Tenant Act 1954 applies.

Prior to the Housing Act 1980, a tenancy of a dwelling with a partial business use could be within the Rent Act as a controlled (but not a regulated) tenancy. Upon the abolition of controlled tenancies by the 1980 Act, these mixed user tenancies became business tenancies within the 1954 Act, which does not require the tenancy to be solely for business purposes.[14]

In order to qualify as a business tenancy (and thereby be excluded from the Rent Act), the tenancy need not have been initially let for business purposes. All that is required is that the tenancy includes premises which are occupied by the tenant for the purposes of a business carried on by him, or for those and other purposes.[15] "Business" is defined as including "a trade, profession or employment," and including "any activity carried on by a body of persons whether corporate or unincorporate."[16]

Clearly a tenancy cannot be within the Rent Act unless, by section 1, it is a tenancy of a house let as a dwelling. So, as we have seen, a letting for business purposes cannot be a protected tenancy even though the tenant uses it for residence.[17] Nor can such a tenancy become protected if the business use is abandoned.[18]

Where a tenancy is initially within the Rent Act, it will cease to be a protected tenancy if a business use develops, unless the business element can be regarded as insignificant. In *Lewis* v. *Weldcrest*[19] the tenant, an elderly woman, took in five lodgers at little or no profit, primarily for company. Whether such an activity was a

[13] s.16A, inserted by H.A. 1980, s.56.
[14] L.T.A. 1954, s.23(1).
[15] *Ibid*. The business user must not be unlawful; s.23(4).
[16] L.T.A. 1954, s.23(2).
[17] *Ponder* v. *Hillman* [1969] 1 W.L.R. 1261, *ante*, p. 15.
[18] *Pulleng* v. *Curran* (1982) 44 P. & C.R. 58, *ante*, p. 15.
[19] [1978] 1 W.L.R. 1107.

"business" was a question of degree, to which decisions on user covenants were not relevant. No single factor was decisive, but the number of lodgers, the money charged and the size of the house were relevant. It was held that the tenant remained within the Rent Act, it being significant that she derived no commercial advantage from the arrangement. Of course, the tenant would continue to have security of tenure even if the tenancy had moved into the business code, but would have had to pay a higher rent, the market rent payable under business tenancies being higher than the Rent Act "fair rent." The result was similar in *Royal Life Saving Society* v. *Page*,[20] where the tenant was a doctor. He used the demised property as his home and had consulting rooms nearby. The landlord agreed that he could see patients at home occasionally. In fact he only saw one or two patients a year there, in emergency. It was held that the business activity was incidental and insignificant, hence it was a protected tenancy. Decided with this case was another, which fell on the other side of the line. In *Cheryl Investments Ltd.* v. *Saldanha*[21] a flat was let to a tenant who was a partner in a business with no trade premises. The tenant worked at home, installing office equipment and receiving frequent business visitors. Although initially within the Rent Acts, as soon as the tenant equipped the premises for business the 1954 Act applied, thereby excluding the Rent Act. Presumably, if the business user had ceased, the tenancy would have become protected again, as it was initially let as a dwelling.

Finally, where the head tenancy is a business tenancy but the property includes residential accommodation, a sub-tenant of the residential part can have a protected tenancy as against the tenant,[22] and may also have rights against the head landlord on termination of the tenancy.[23]

(p) Parsonage houses

Church of England parsonage houses are excluded from the Rent Act, not by express provision in the latter, but by virtue of the Pluralities Act 1838.[24] There is no such exception in respect of

---

[20] [1978] 1 W.L.R. 1329.
[21] *Ibid.* The business user was apparently not in breach of covenant. See also *Groveside Properties Ltd.* v. *Westminster Medical School* (1983) 47 P. & C.R. 507, *ante*, p. 27.
[22] R.A. 1977, s.24(3).
[23] *Ibid.* s.137(3), *post*, p. 128.
[24] See *Bishop of Gloucester* v. *Cunningham* [1943] 1 K.B. 101. The general provisions of the 1977 Act do not detract from the specific provisions of the 1838 Act.

other denominations, although the 1977 Act provides a ground for possession of a regulated tenancy where the dwelling is held for the purpose of being available for occupation by a minister of religion, and is required for such occupation.[25]

(q) Exemption by ministerial order

Finally, section 143(1) of the 1977 Act provides that the Secretary of State may by order provide that dwelling-houses in a particular area shall not be the subject of a regulated tenancy if he is satisfied that the number of persons seeking to become tenants is not substantially greater than the number of dwelling-houses available. Any such order may contain transitional provisions to avoid or mitigate hardship. No such order has yet been made.

---

[25] R.A. 1977, Sched. 15, para. 15.

Chapter 3

RESIDENT LANDLORDS

Prior to the Rent Act 1974 the general position was that tenants of unfurnished premises were protected while tenants of furnished premises were not. One justification for this was that the Act should always provide for a class of unprotected tenants in order to encourage letting. In any event the classification was not entirely arbitrary, as the tenant who had furnished the premises himself would be more greatly disadvantaged by lack of security than the more mobile tenant of furnished premises. However, the ease with which landlords could furnish premises and thus avoid the Act[1] led to a need for a more rational distinction between protected and unprotected tenants. The result was the Rent Act 1974, bringing furnished tenants into protection and introducing the distinction between tenants of resident and non-resident landlords. This, it was hoped, would encourage owners to let any rooms in their homes which they did not require, in the knowledge that the tenants would not have full security of tenure. That full security would be inappropriate in such circumstances is self-evident. As it was said in *Bardrick* v. *Haycock,*[2] "the mischief at which the section was aimed was the mischief of that sort of social embarrassment arising out of close proximity."

The present provisions are contained in section 12 and Schedule 2 of the 1977 Act, as amended by section 65 of the Housing Act 1980.

It should be noted that the concept of sharing accommodation[3] is not relevant to the resident landlord rules, which may be satisfied even if no rooms are shared.

The Statutory Conditions[4]

Tenancies granted on or after August 14, 1974 are not protected if the following conditions are all satisfied:

---

[1] Prior to the decision in *Woodward* v. *Docherty* [1974] 1 W.L.R. 966, *infra.*
[2] (1976) 31 P. & C.R. 420 at 424.
[3] *Ante*, p. 18.
[4] R.A. 1977, s.12(1), as amended by H.A. 1980, s.65. It seems that the landlord need own no interest in the building; Farrand and Arden, *Rent Acts and Regulations* (2nd ed.), p. 49.

(*a*) *The dwelling-house forms part only of a building and, except in a case where the dwelling-house also forms part of a flat, the building is not a purpose-built block of flats*

A "flat" is a dwelling which forms part only of a building and is separated horizontally from another dwelling forming part of the same building; a "purpose-built block of flats" is one which as constructed contained (and contains) two or more flats.[5]

The rationale of this requirement is that if a landlord owns several flats in a block, living in one and letting the others, he is not within the policy of the resident landlord exception, as he is not sharing his house in any real sense. The original provision was modified by section 65 of the Housing Act 1980 (as to tenancies granted on or after November 28, 1980), so that the condition may be satisfied in the case of an individual flat in a purpose-built block which the landlord lives in and has let off in part to a tenant: such a case is within the policy of the resident landlord exception.

The meaning of "purpose-built" arose in *Barnes* v. *Gorsuch*,[6] where a Victorian house, later converted to flats, did not satisfy the definition. "As constructed" means as originally constructed. The conversion did not start the construction anew. On the facts, there was no ground for saying that the identity of the building had changed, although the possibility of such an argument was admitted, for example in a case where the property was completely gutted and rebuilt inside. As to the "close proximity" principle,[7] it was agreed that people cannot always lead separate lives without "social embarrassment" even in a purpose-built block, and that sometimes in conversions they can. But the conditions exclude purpose-built blocks because they are likely to be places where the occupiers lead separate lives.

(*b*) *At the grant of the tenancy the landlord occupied as his residence another dwelling forming part of the building*[8]

"Building"is not defined in the Act. No doubt it does not include adjoining terraced houses or a pair of semi-detached houses, which would not be within the policy of the rule. In any case a statutory definition is unlikely to have resolved the borderline cases which follow.[9]

---

[5] *Ibid.* Sched. 2, para. 4.
[6] (1982) 43 P. & C.R. 294.
[7] *Bardrick* v. *Haycock, supra.*
[8] Or, in the case of a flat in a purpose-built block, forming part of the flat.
[9] See the volume of litigation on the statutory definition of "house" in the Leasehold Reform Act 1967.

In *Bardrick* v. *Haycock*[10] a house was converted to flats. The landlord pulled down an adjoining garage and built an extension, having its own front door, where he resided. This was held not to be "part of the building," hence the tenants were protected. This decision was applied in principle by the Court of Appeal in *Griffiths* v. *English*,[11] but a different conclusion was reached on basically similar facts. The main house was divided into flats. There was a single storey extension at either side, with no communicating door. The landlord, who lived in one extension, was held to be a resident landlord. This is a question of fact for the judge at first instance to decide. The appellate court will interfere only if he has erred in law, and not if, as here, it is a borderline case where different views can reasonably be held.

Even where there is no dispute as to the "building," questions can arise as to whether the landlord occupies another dwelling-house in that building as his residence. In *Lyons* v. *Caffery*[12] a basement contained a bed-sitter, kitchen, bathroom and sunroom. The bedsitter was let to a tenant, who shared the kitchen[13] and bathroom with the landlord, who occupied the remainder. It was held that the resident landlord condition was not satisfied. The essential living and sleeping room was let and the remainder was not a dwelling-house. This emphasis on sleeping facilities is clearly consistent with decisions on "dwelling-house" and "residence" in sections 1 and 2 of the Act.[14]

(c) At all times since the grant of the tenancy the landlord (or his successor) has occupied as his residence another dwelling forming part of the building[15]

The landlord is treated as occupying as a residence if he fulfills the same conditions as a statutory tenant must fulfill under section 2 of the Act.[16] Hence the case law on the statutory tenancy[17]

[10] (1976) 31 P. & C.R. 420 (C.A.).
[11] (1982) 261 E.G. 257; [1983] Conv. 147 (J.E.M.).
[12] (1983) 266 E.G. 213 (C.A.).
[13] Why, then, was the tenant not excluded from protection on the ground that he shared "living accommodation" with the landlord? (*Ante,* p. 18.)
[14] See *Regalian Securities Ltd.* v. *Scheuer* (1982) 263 E.G. 973 (s.2); *Curl* v. *Angelo* [1948] 2 All E.R. 189 (s.1).
[15] Or, in the case of a flat in a purpose-built block, forming part of the flat. The condition is satisfied where the landlord's interest is held on trust and the beneficiary resides; Sched. 2, para. 2.
[16] Sched. 2, para. 5. Thus a company cannot be a resident landlord.
[17] *Post,* p. 55.

applies here also. One perhaps unforeseen consequence of this is that liberal decisions favouring the tenant, for example the "two homes" cases,[18] can here be utilised by the landlord. It cannot have been the intention of Parliament that the resident landlord exception could be relied on in respect of more than one property or in cases involving lengthy absence from the premises. So far there is little authority in this area.

However, the question of joint landlords has been resolved. In *Cooper* v. *Tait*[19] the Court of Appeal held that residence by one of joint landlords satisfied the condition. This is clearly satisfactory, as absurd and unjust results would flow from any other view, for example if a married couple let the property and then separated.

The "Period of Disregard"

Clearly continuous residence cannot be expected, as the landlord will ultimately die or sell the property, and his successor cannot always practicably take up occupation immediately. Hence the thread of occupation by the landlord is preserved by the provision of "periods of disregard." Basically a period of 28 days (extendable to six months by giving notice) may be disregarded in the case of a life-time transfer, while the period is two years where the landlord's interest becomes vested in personal representatives, "trustees as such" or the Probate Judge (*i.e.* prior to the appointment of administrators on intestacy).[20] The provisions are complex and badly drafted, and have troubled the Court of Appeal and House of Lords on several occasions.

(i) Personal representatives

Here the provisions have been amended by the Housing Act, but the position prior to the amendment must be considered, as the interpretation of the original provisions continues to have relevance in the cases of purchasers and trustees, discussed below.

(a) Position prior to the Housing Act 1980
In determining whether condition (c) was fulfilled, the 1977 Act provided that a period not exceeding 12 months while the land-

---

[18] *Post,* p. 62.
[19] (1984) 271 E.G. 105. See also (on Case 11) *Tilling* v. *Whiteman* [1980] A.C. 1 and (on joint tenants) *Lloyd* v. *Sadler* [1978] Q.B. 774.
[20] Sched. 2, para. 1, as amended by H.A. 1980, s.65.

lord's interest was vested in personal representatives could be disregarded. Clearly the tenant would become protected if no notice was served during this period, and no successor took up residence by the end of it. But what if (assuming a periodic tenancy) notice was served during this period? The matter arose in *Landau* v. *Sloane*.[21] A majority of the House of Lords, reversing the Court of Appeal, held that the personal representatives could recover possession after the 12 month period even though no successor had gone into residence. The purpose of the rule was to give them the same rights as the landlord. Otherwise there would be no inducement to let, as it would be unjust to the estate if the tenant became protected. The house would often be the most valuable asset in the estate, and the successor would not normally wish to reside. What of the tenant's status during this period? Not surprisingly, he was not a trespasser. He was a person holding over, against whom no order for possession could be made save on grounds that would terminate a regulated tenancy.[22] Thus the personal representatives had the same rights as a resident landlord, save that they could not recover possession until the end of the period of disregard. Lord Roskill dissented, considering that the resident landlord status was a privilege that was lost if the conditions were not satisfied, the conditions requiring residence at all times save in the period of disregard.

A final point concerning this decision is that, while agreeing that a contractual tenancy would become protected if not terminated during the period of disregard, the House of Lords suggested that it would be an abuse of power if a Rent Tribunal postponed the operation of a notice to quit merely to create this result.[23]

This subsequently arose in *Williams* v. *Mate*.[24] Personal representatives of a deceased resident landlord gave notice to quit, but the Rent Tribunal postponed its operation beyond the period of disregard. As no beneficiary had taken up occupation, the tenant became a statutory tenant.[25] Thus the tenant gained protection solely by the action of the Rent Tribunal, which, however, was not taken deliberately to deprive the landlord of his rights.

---

[21] [1982] A.C. 490, criticised [1981] Conv. 225 (A. Sydenham).
[22] Sched. 2, para. 3 (this restriction no longer applies to personal representatives after the 1980 amendment, *infra*).
[23] This cannot be done in the case of tenancies granted after the Housing Act 1980. See R.A. 1977, ss.103–106; H.A. 1980, s.69.
[24] (1983) 46 P. & C.R. 43 (C.A.).
[25] Sched. 2, para. 7 (which was described as obscurely drafted).

(*b*) *Effect of Housing Act 1980, section 65*

The rule discussed above was amended in two respects. First, the 12 month period was extended to two years. Secondly, and presumably in response to the Court of Appeal decision in *Landau* v. *Sloane*, it is now provided that condition (c) (the continuous residence rule) is deemed satisfied during this two-year period. The result of this is that the personal representatives can actually recover possession after serving notice to quit without waiting until the end of the two-year period, and without establishing grounds to terminate a regulated tenancy. This aspect of the amendment applies only to deaths after November 28, 1980, but difficult questions have arisen as to the retrospective operation of the provision extending the period from 12 months to two years.

This was the issue before the Court of Appeal in *Caldwell* v. *McAteer*.[26] It had already been suggested in *Williams* v. *Mate* that section 65 was retrospective in the sense that personal representatives could take advantage of the extended period even where the 12 month period had expired before section 65 came into operation, provided the tenancy had not already became statutory.[27] In *Caldwell* v. *McAteer* the landlord died on October 31, 1979. After the (then) 12 month period of disregard, the tenant became protected, no beneficiary having gone into residence. If notice to quit had been given subsequently but prior to the coming into operation of section 65, the tenancy would have become statutory. However, section 65 came into operation on November 28, 1980, and extended the 12 month period to two years. Within the two-year period, the personal representatives gave notice to quit (expiring October 17, 1981). It was held that section 65 applied retrospectively, thus enabling the personal representatives to recover possession at the end of the two-year period. It was admitted that the result was anomalous and the Act ill-drafted, but denied that this construction deprived the tenant of a vested right, as no statutory tenancy had yet arisen. This, it is submitted, is unconvincing. It is difficult to think of other examples where protected tenants have been retrospectively deprived of that status. The basic characteristic of a protected tenancy is the right to a statutory tenancy. Some retrospective effect could have been given to section 65 by applying it to cases where the "period of disregard" was already running, but the tenant had not yet acquired a

---

[26] (1984) 269 E.G. 1039; [1985] Conv. 127 (J.E.M.).
[27] The tenancy would have become statutory if no notice was served until after the 12 month period (no beneficiary having gone into residence).

protected tenancy because the period had not expired when section 65 came into effect.

(ii) Purchasers[28]

The 1977 Act provided for a period of disregard of 14 days, now increased to 28 days by the Act of 1980. If, during this period, the purchaser gives written notice to the tenant of his intention to reside in the building, the period may be extended to six months. Thus if the contractual tenancy does not terminate during this period, the tenant becomes protected if the purchaser has not moved in by the end of the period of disregard. If a notice to quit has been served during this period, then presumably the reasoning of *Landau* v. *Sloane*[29] continues to apply, as the 1980 Act only enables personal representatives to recover possession during the period.[30] Hence the purchaser can recover possession at the end of the period even if he has not moved in.[31]

It should be noted that the period of disregard starts running only on completion of the purchase. The purchaser cannot give his "extension notice" until the property is legally vested in him. Thus difficulties may arise if the vendor has moved out before completion.[32]

(iii) "Trustees as such" (or the Probate Judge)

The 12-month period originally provided was increased by the 1980 Act to two years, but that Act made no further amendment here. Thus the position is in principle similar to that of the purchaser, discussed above. Possession can be recovered after the period of disregard if notice to quit has been served within it, even though no successor has gone into occupation. If the contractual tenancy has not terminated within the period the tenant becomes protected in the absence of occupation by a successor by the end of the period.

The difficulty is as to the precise scope of the phrase "trustees as such." There is, as yet, no direct authority, but it was suggested in *Williams* v. *Mate*[33] that it is not confined to an *inter vivos* trust, but

[28] The category in fact comprises any life-time transfer.
[29] *Supra.*
[30] Although, by Sched. 2, para. 3, the purchaser may do so by establishing a ground which would terminate a regulated tenancy.
[31] What if his intention to reside was not genuine?
[32] See [1978] Conv. 255 (J.T.F.), discussing whether such an interval of non-occupation before completion could, if short, be disregarded as *de minimis,* or whether the express periods of disregard preclude this.
[33] *Supra.*

applies to trustees under a will or intestacy. Where the property vests first in a personal representative and then in trustees, the two periods of disregard are not mutually exclusive but can be added.[34]

Finally, even if conditions (a), (b) and (c) are all satisfied, it should be noted that the resident landlord rules do not apply to a tenancy granted to a person who, immediately before the grant, was a protected or statutory tenant of that dwelling or another dwelling in the building.[35] Thus a tenant, once protected, cannot lose his status by the grant of a new tenancy by a resident landlord.

The Transitional Provisions

Where a furnished letting was granted by a resident landlord before August 14, 1974, then, so long as the landlord was resident on that date (and thereafter), the tenant is not protected. If, however, the letting was unfurnished, then the resident landlord rules do not apply.[36] We have seen that tenancies granted on or after that date by resident landlords are unprotected whether or not furnished.

The rationale of these rules is that furnished tenants were unprotected before the 1974 Act, and so lost nothing by continuing unprotected, while unfurnished tenants were protected even if the landlord was resident, and should not be retrospectively deprived of their status.[37]

In the case of an unfurnished letting before the 1974 Act it is important to notice that, while the resident landlord rule does not apply, the tenant will nevertheless fail to be fully protected if he shares "living accommodation" with his landlord.[38]

While the distinction between furnished and unfurnished tenancies has lost its primary significance since the 1974 Act, it will be seen that in the context of the transitional provisions[39] it is still necessary to determine whether or not a tenancy is furnished. It will be convenient to consider this matter here.

---

[34] See further Farrand and Arden, *Rent Acts and Regulations* (2nd ed.), p. 48, and Pettit, *Private Sector Tenancies* (2nd ed.) pp. 58–59, canvassing further difficulties in the interpretation of "trustees as such."

[35] R.A. 1977, s.12(2), as amended.

[36] *Ibid.* Sched. 24, para. 6.

[37] See *Christophides* v. *Cuming* (1976) 239 E.G. 275; *Mann* v. *Cornella* (1980) 254 E.G. 403.

[38] *Ibid.* s.21, *ante,* p. 18. Such a tenant has a restricted contract, *post,* p. 110.

[39] And in some others, *e.g.* s.138, *post,* p. 129, (subtenancies). The definition of a restricted contract in s.19 also includes furniture, but there it need not be a substantial element.

What is a Furnished Tenancy?

By section 152 of the 1977 Act the definition of a furnished tenancy (whether regulated, protected or statutory) is one where the dwelling-house is bona fide[40] let at a rent which includes payments in respect of furniture, and in respect of which the amount of rent fairly attributable to the use of furniture, having regard to the value of that use to the tenant, forms a substantial part of the whole rent.

Much of the case-law concerns the pre-1974 law, but remains relevant. The leading case is *Palser* v. *Grinling*,[41] favouring a broad approach to the meaning of "substantial."

The significance of the requirement of substantiality can be seen in *Woodward* v. *Docherty*,[42] where a flat was let "fully furnished," with all the tenant could require. The rent was £520 per annum. The furniture was second-hand and worth about £100, representing about £40 per annum of the rent. It was held that a broad approach should be taken, bearing in mind that second-hand furniture is cheaply available. The tenancy was held unfurnished for Rent Act purposes, as £40 was not a substantial part of the rent. This was followed in *Christophides* v. *Cuming*,[43] where a flat was held unfurnished, even though the tenant had all he required and both parties regarded it as furnished. The furniture element was about 7 per cent. of the rent, which was not substantial. It was suggested that 14 per cent. would be borderline.

An initially furnished tenancy can change to unfurnished by agreement or fundamental change,[44] but a gradual replacement with the tenant's furniture does not suffice.[45] It may be relevant that the tenant has previously referred the rent to the Rent Tribunal on the basis of a furnished tenancy.[46]

Status of a Tenant of a Resident Landlord

Finally, it remains to consider the position of a tenant deprived of full protection by the resident landlord rules. While he cannot

---

[40] *i.e.* the term as to furniture must not be a sham; see *Palser* v. *Grinling* [1948] A.C. 291.
[41] *Supra.*
[42] [1974] 1 W.L.R. 966.
[43] *Supra.*
[44] *Seabrook* v. *Mervyn* [1947] 1 All E.R. 295.
[45] *Klassnick* v. *Allen* [1969] 1 W.L.R. 1616.
[46] *Goel* v. *Sagoo* [1970] 1 Q.B. 1; *cf. Thomas* v. *Pascal* [1969] 1 W.L.R. 1475.

have a regulated tenancy, the tenant does have the protection of a restricted contract.[47] Briefly, this means that rent control applies, but not security of tenure. The position differs according to whether the tenancy was granted before or after the Housing Act 1980. In the latter case the tenant cannot be evicted without a court order, which may be suspended for up to three months.[48]

[47] *Post,* Chap. 8.
[48] H.A. 1980, s.69.

Chapter 4

ASSURED AND SHORTHOLD TENANCIES

These two types of tenancies are new concepts, introduced by the Housing Act 1980 with a view to encouraging new lettings. Shorthold tenancies are protected tenancies within the Rent Act, although they do not have all the attributes of the normal protected tenancy. Assured tenancies, on the other hand, are excluded from Rent Act protection. It is, therefore, somewhat of a digression to include them here. They will be discussed (briefly) in order to illustrate the scheme of the 1980 Act to ease the shortage of rented accommodation, and to assess how far that scheme has succeeded.

Assured Tenancies

By section 56 of the 1980 Act, a tenancy under which a dwelling-house is let as a separate dwelling is an assured tenancy and not a housing association tenancy or a protected tenancy if (a) it would, when created, have been a protected or housing association tenancy but for this section, and (b) the following three conditions are satisfied:

(i) The interest of the landlord has, since the creation of the tenancy, belonged to an approved body.

(ii) The dwelling-house is, or forms part of, a building which was erected (and on which construction work first began) after the passing of the Act.

(iii) Before the tenant first occupied the dwelling-house under the tenancy, no part of it had been occupied by any person as his residence except under an assured tenancy.

An "approved body" is a body, or one of a description of bodies, specified for this purpose by an order made by the Secretary of State.[1] Many of these approved bodies are housing

---

[1] There are now almost 200 approved landlords, and about 500 assured tenancies; (1986) 277 E.G. 1182. Details of recent Orders can be found at [1985] Conv. 442.

associations, pension funds or financial institutions. Such bodies are not however, obliged to grant assured tenancies. By section 56(6), any tenancy granted by an approved body may instead be a protected (or housing association) tenancy if, before the grant, the landlord gave the tenant a notice in prescribed form[2] to that effect.

The effect of condition (i) above is that the tenancy ceases to be assured (and becomes a protected or housing association tenancy) if the landlord ceases to be an approved body. This is qualified in two respects by section 57. If the loss of status occurs by reason only of a variation in the bodies or descriptions of bodies for the time being specified as approved bodies, then any tenancy already granted (or any further tenancy to a person in possession as an assured tenant immediately before the grant[3]) continues to be assured. If for any other reason the interest of the landlord has ceased to belong to an approved body (for example, by assignment), a period not exceeding three months is disregarded in determining whether condition (i) is satisfied. In such a case of a transfer to a non-approved body, the tenancy continues to be assured for three months, and thereafter becomes a protected (or housing association) tenancy. In view of the security régime (discussed below) applicable to assured tenancies, it is unlikely that the transferee landlord will be able to recover possession during this three-month period. If the reversion is transferred to a landlord which is an approved body within the three months, the tenancy is assured throughout.

Security and rent are dealt with by section 58 and Schedule 5. Broadly, the statutory scheme for business tenants embodied in Part II of the Landlord and Tenant Act 1954 is made applicable to assured tenancies, with such modifications as are necessary to reflect the fact that such tenancies are residential. The effect of this, in outline, is that the tenancy continues after termination of the contractual term until properly determined in accordance with the Act. If the parties fail to renew the tenancy by agreement, the tenant is entitled to seek renewal by the court, upon such terms as the court directs. There is no control of the rent payable under the initial tenancy, nor under any renewal by agreement. If the tenancy is renewed by the court, the market rent will be payable, as fixed by the court. The landlord may apply for an interim rent (higher than the contractual rent) pending the grant of the

---

[2] Assured Tenancies (Notice to Tenant) Regulations 1981 (S.I. 1981 No. 591).

[3] *i.e.* where the tenancy is renewed under the security régime of the L.T.A. 1954, Part II, discussed below.

renewed tenancy. The landlord can oppose renewal on various grounds, but must compensate the tenant where the grounds are not based on the tenant's default. The compensation is, however, lower in the case of assured tenants than in the case of business tenants,[4] presumably because the element of loss of goodwill is not present.

It has been suggested that an assured tenancy could also qualify as a restricted contract (assuming furniture or services were provided), in which case there would be a conflict between the Rent Tribunal's jurisdiction as to the rent and the market rent provisions noted above.[5]

It will be appreciated that the purpose of these new provisions was to provide an incentive to invest in the building of new residential accommodation for private letting. There would be no such incentive if the tenancies would be within the Rent Act, as the "fair rent" there obtainable provides a lower return on capital in comparison with other investments. The compromise offered by the assured tenancy is that the tenant has security but must pay the market rent.[6] Such is the scheme of the business tenancy code, which has not deterred lettings in that sector.

There have been gloomy predictions for the assured tenancy.[7] The scheme should, however, receive a boost if an amendment contained in the Housing and Planning Bill is enacted. Assured tenancies will no longer be confined to newly-built property. The Bill extends the scheme to empty property which has been substantially improved, repaired or converted, provided the landlord is an "approved body."

Protected Shorthold Tenancies

As their name indicates, protected shorthold tenancies are protected tenancies within the Rent Act. Although subject to rent control, they do not enjoy the full measure of security of tenure which is the characteristic of other protected tenancies. This is because, on termination, the landlord is entitled to invoke a man-

---

[4] H.A. 1980, Sched. 5, para. 7. The rules are also different as to contracting out of compensation; *ibid.* para. 8.
[5] Farrand and Arden, *Rent Acts and Regulations* (2nd ed.), p. 322.
[6] Although this might be difficult to assess in the absence of "comparables."
[7] Yates and Hawkins, *Landlord and Tenant Law* (1981), p. 374. See also (1985) 276 E.G. 1147 (M. Boléat), suggesting that the abolition of capital allowances as part of corporation tax reform has caused a severe setback to the assured tenancy scheme.

datory ground for possession. Of course, as we will see, there are other mandatory grounds for possession, such as the "owner-occupier" ground (Case 11[8]), but not all landlords can bring themselves within their requirements. This lack of full security would, it was hoped, provide the incentive to let property in the private sector.

(i) Definition of a shorthold tenancy

By section 52 of the Housing Act 1980, a protected shorthold tenancy is one granted after the Act for a term certain of one to five years, satisfying the following conditions:

(a) it cannot be terminated by the landlord before expiry save by forfeiture for non-payment of rent or breach of any other obligation in the tenancy; and

(b) before the grant the landlord gave the tenant a notice in prescribed form[9] stating that the tenancy is to be a protected shorthold tenancy; and

(c) either the rent for the dwelling-house is registered[10] at the grant of the tenancy, or a certificate of fair rent[11] has been issued in respect of the dwelling-house and the rent under the tenancy does not exceed the rent specified in the certificate, and an application to register the rent is made not later than 28 days after the beginning of the term and is not withdrawn.

Condition (c), by order of the Secretary of State,[12] is now confined to tenancies in Greater London. In other areas, the tenant can still of course, apply for a registered rent, but registration is no longer a condition of the shorthold tenancy.

Even where conditions (b) or (c) are not satisfied, the landlord may still invoke the mandatory ground for possession, discussed below, if the court is of the opinion that it is just and equitable to make an order for possession.[13] Similar dispensing powers exist in

---

[8] *Post*, p. 82.
[9] Protected Shorthold Tenancies (Notice to Tenant) Regulations 1981 (S.I. 1981 No. 1579).
[10] *Post*, p. 137.
[11] *Post*, p. 146.
[12] Under s.52(4); Protected Shorthold Tenancies (Rent Registration) Order 1981 (S.I. 1981 No. 1578).
[13] H.A. 1980, s.55(2).

relation to certain other grounds for possession, and it may be that decisions in those areas may provide guidance in the present context.[14] It is not clear whether the dispensing power is exercisable where both conditions are unsatisfied.

The tenancy must, in all other respects, qualify as a protected tenancy. A protected shorthold tenancy cannot be granted to a person who, immediately before the grant, was a protected or statutory tenant of the dwelling-house.[15]

It will be seen that the shorthold tenancy is, in effect, a compromise. As stated above, the incentive to the landlord lies in the lack of full security. To protect the tenant, this is balanced by the fact that he must have a contractual term of at least a year[16] and that, in London, he must have the benefit of a registered rent.[17] These two factors are not present in an ordinary protected tenancy.

Although the effect of condition (a) is that the landlord cannot terminate the tenancy prematurely save by forfeiture, section 53 permits the tenant to terminate it (notwithstanding anything in the terms of the tenancy) by written notice to the landlord. The notice must be one month if the term does not exceed two years, otherwise three months. Any agreement, whether or not contained in the instrument creating the tenancy, is void in so far as it purports to impose a penalty or disability on the tenant in the event of such a notice.

(ii) Assignment and sub-letting

These are governed by the somewhat complex rules contained in section 54. A protected shorthold tenancy and any protected tenancy of the same dwelling-house granted during the "continuous period," specified below, shall not be "capable of assignment," except in pursuance of a court order under section 24 of the Matrimonial Causes Act 1973, *i.e.* on divorce.

The "continuous period" begins on the grant of the protected shorthold tenancy and continues until either no person is in pos-

---

[14] See particularly the authorities on Case 11, *post,* p. 85.

[15] H.A. 1980, s.52(2).

[16] It is doubtful whether the term could be granted retrospectively. Although this is possible at common law (see *Bradshaw* v. *Pawley* [1980] 1 W.L.R. 10), this would be an evasion of the requirements.

[17] The view of the Opposition when the registration requirement was lifted outside London was that this destroyed the "central structure" of shortholds; *Hansard,* Vol. 10, col. 678 (October 26, 1981). It appears that the majority of shortholds are outside London; [1982] Conv. 29 at pp. 34–35 (P. F. Smith).

session as a protected or statutory tenant, or a protected tenancy is granted to a person who is not, immediately before the grant, in possession of the dwelling-house as a protected or statutory tenant. In effect, this is the same period as that during which the landlord has the right to invoke the mandatory ground for possession, discussed below.

In the case of the ordinary covenant against assignment under the general law, it is well established that the lease can be effectively assigned at law, the consequence of the prohibition being simply that a breach of covenant has occurred, usually resulting in a liability to forfeiture.[18] The wording of section 54, however, indicates that a purported assignment could not be effective to transfer the tenancy.[19] This is so whether or not the tenancy itself contains a covenant against assignment. Possibly an assignment by operation of law can be effective, for example, to a trustee in bankruptcy or to the personal representative on the death of the shorthold tenant.[20] This is another feature which distinguishes the shorthold from an ordinary protected tenancy, which may be assigned unless there is a prohibition in the tenancy itself.

There is, on the other hand, no statutory restriction on subletting (although, of course, the tenancy itself may prohibit it). Where there is a sub-letting of the whole or part of the dwelling-house let under a shorthold tenancy at any time during the "continuous period" mentioned above, section 54(1) provides that if the landlord becomes entitled to possession against the tenant during that period, then he shall also be entitled as against the sub-tenant.[21] It is not clear whether this provision precludes the sub-tenant from relying on any common law rights he may have, for example if the head tenancy ends by forfeiture or surrender.

(iii) Recovery of possession

Because the shorthold is a protected tenancy, the normal consequences of a protected tenancy, such as its transition to a statutory tenancy on termination and the possibility of succession rights, follow if the landlord does not seek possession. The characteristic of

---

[18] See *Old Grovebury Manor Farm* v. *Seymour (W.) Plant Sales and Hire* [1979] 1 W.L.R. 263.
[19] Compare the wording of H.A. 1985, s. 91 (secure tenancies).
[20] The tenancy would not, however, be assignable in the hands of such assignees by operation of law.
[21] For the general position in the case of sub-tenancies, see s.137, *post*, p. 120.

a shorthold tenancy, however, is that the landlord may invoke a mandatory ground for possession. Section 55 of the 1980 Act introduces Case 19 into the Rent Act grounds for possession. This right to possession arises where the dwelling-house has been let on a shorthold tenancy, and either there has been no grant of a further tenancy of the dwelling-house since the termination of the short-hold tenancy, or, if there was such a grant, it was to a person who immediately before the grant was in possession as a protected or statutory tenant. This refers to the former shorthold tenant (or his successor on death) holding over under a new contractual tenancy or under a statutory tenancy. The landlord must commence proceedings for possession after notice to the tenant and not later than 3 months after expiry of the notice. The notice must be written and must state that proceedings for possession may be brought under Case 19 after its expiry. The rules as to the timing of this notice are somewhat complicated.[22] It must expire not earlier than 3 months after it is served. If the tenancy is periodic at this time,[23] it must not expire before the tenancy could be ended by a notice to quit served on the same day. The notice must be served in the period of 3 months immediately preceding the date on which the protected shorthold tenancy comes to an end, or, if that date has passed, in the period of 3 months immediately preceding any anniversary of that date. It must not be served earlier than 3 months after the expiry of any previous valid notice (which has lapsed). We have already seen that the court may dispense with the conditions relating to registered rent or to notice before the grant stating that the tenancy is shorthold, which should be satisfied if the tenancy is to qualify as shorthold, if it is just and equitable to make a possession order.

The effect of these rules is that the landlord is not obliged to seek possession at the earliest opportunity. Failure to do so does not prejudice his right to invoke Case 19 at a later stage. The right to possession may be asserted against the original tenant who is holding over after expiry as a statutory tenant, or against a member of his family who succeeded to the tenancy on death. Case 19 continues to apply where a new tenancy, fixed or periodic, is granted to the former shorthold tenant or his successor after the shorthold tenancy ends. The later tenancy is not shorthold,[24] but the landlord's rights are preserved.

---

[22] For some of the difficulties, see [1982] Conv. 29 at 41–42 (P. F. Smith); Yates and Hawkins, *Landlord and Tenant Law,* p. 372.
[23] See s.52(5).
[24] s.52(2), (5); Case 19, para. (a).

(iv) Conclusion

At the time of writing it cannot be said that the introduction of the shorthold tenancy has achieved the aim of easing the shortage of rented accommodation. In 1981 the Government admitted that the experiment was unsuccessful.[25] The difficulty is that the Labour Party has declared its intention to repeal these provisions if it returns to power, retrospectively conferring full security of shorthold tenants.[26] Landlords are accordingly unlikely to be influenced by the advantages of the shorthold tenancy. The legislation, it has been said,

> "is marred by the sheer complexity of the formal provisions. Owing to the danger of repeal it might therefore be best to advise landlords, if they avail themselves of shortholds, to let for the shortest possible time and to seek to recover possession without hesitation at the earliest available moment."[27]

Similarly, "it seems unlikely that many new landlords will be attracted to the housing market, though it may well be that a person who was intending to let or re-let in any event will now prefer to do so by creating a protected shorthold tenancy."[28]

[25] See *The Times,* March 11, 1981, stating that only 320 such tenancies were known to exist in the country. By August 1981 there were 3,500 shortholds known to the Department of the Environment, but up to 50,000 properties empty due to the Rent Act; *Hansard,* Vol. 10, col. 675 (October 26, 1981); *cf. The Times,* February 21, 1986, estimating over half a million empty properties.

[26] *Hansard,* H.C., Committee F, col. 1180 (March 18, 1980); *Hansard,* Vol. 10, col. 681 (October 26, 1981).

[27] [1982] Conv. 29, at p. 42 (P. F. Smith).

[28] Pettit, *Private Sector Tenancies* (2nd ed.), p. 36. See also (1985) 275 E.G. 771 at 774 (G. Martin and T. Crook), for a more encouraging view.

Chapter 5

THE STATUTORY TENANCY

Section 2 of the 1977 Act provides that "after the termination of a protected tenancy of a dwelling-house the person who, immediately before that termination, was the protected tenant of the dwelling-house shall, if and so long as he occupies the dwelling-house as his residence, be the statutory tenant of it."

The matters to be considered in this chapter include the juridical nature of the statutory tenancy, the meaning of the words "if and so long as he occupies the dwelling-house as his residence," and the terms of the statutory tenancy.

Nature of the Statutory Tenancy[1]

The statutory tenancy, unlike the protected tenancy which preceded it, is neither a legal estate nor an equitable interest in the land. It does, however, have some of the attributes of a proprietary interest. It might best be described as a hybrid interest created by statute, in some respects personal to the tenant, in others proprietary in nature.

Although not an interest in land in the accepted sense, the statutory tenancy is clearly binding on third parties, including purchasers, who acquire the landlord's interest. In describing the status of the statutory tenant, Scrutton L.J. said "I take it that he has a right as against all the world to remain in possession until he is turned out by an order of the Court . . . "[2] The binding effect of the tenancy stems not from the characteristics of any legal or equitable interest (which, as stated above, it is not), but from the provisions of the Act. There is, however, an exception to the rule that the tenancy binds "all the world." A mortgagor may grant a tenancy although his mortgage excludes the power of leasing. Any such tenancy will, of course, bind the mortgagor, but will not bind the mortgagee (unless he accepts the tenant), whose title is paramount.[3]

---

[1] See generally [1980] Conv. 351 (C. Hand).
[2] *Keeves* v. *Dean* [1924] 1 K.B. 685 at 694. See also *Jessamine Investment Co.* v. *Schwartz* [1978] Q.B. 264, *post,* p. 130.
[3] *Dudley and District Benefit Building Society* v. *Emerson* [1949] Ch. 707, *post,* p. 132; *cf. Quennell* v. *Maltby* [1979] 1 W.L.R. 318. For the view that a statutory tenancy can be binding on such a mortgagee, see (1977) 41 Conv. (N.S.) 197 (P. Smith); *cf.* correspondence at [1978] Conv. 322.

The statutory tenant, then, is entitled to enjoy possession of the property until he decides to terminate the tenancy or the landlord successfully asserts a ground for possession against him. As with any other tenancy, his right to possession gives him the right to maintain an action in trespass against third parties. Unlike other tenancies. however, he must satisfy the residence requirements (discussed below) in order to keep his tenancy alive. The statutory tenancy clearly has a monetary value. Although the tenant cannot assign it for a premium[4] (or, generally, at all), he may receive payment from the landlord as a condition of giving up possession.[5]

The reason why the statutory tenancy is often described as merely a personal right to occupy is primarily because it is not assignable. An ordinary tenancy is assignable, but may be subject to a prohibition in the terms of the tenancy. A statutory tenancy, on the other hand, is not capable of assignment. To this rule there are two exceptions: the court may order a transfer of the tenancy in matrimonial proceedings,[6] and the landlord may agree to a transfer of the statutory tenancy to a third party.[7] This limited transmissibility of the statutory tenancy has the following, perhaps anomalous, result. If a protected tenant goes bankrupt, his tenancy vests in his trustee in bankruptcy, with the effect that, on disclaimer, the former tenant loses his rights.[8] If, on the other hand, a statutory tenant goes bankrupt, there is no transfer of his tenancy to his trustee in bankruptcy, and hence no loss of Rent Act rights.[9]

Nor can the statutory tenancy be left by will, although, as we will see, two statutory transmissions may take place in favour of members of the family of the deceased tenant.[10]

A statutory tenant may, however, sublet part of the premises, even though he has no "estate" out of which to sublet.[11] If, on the other hand, he sublets the whole of the premises, then although a valid sub-tenancy is created,[12] the act of subletting causes the

---

[4] *Post,* p. 155.
[5] R.A. 1977, Sched. 1, para. 12. The tenant commits an offence if he receives payment from any person other than the landlord.
[6] *Post,* p. 67.
[7] R.A. 1977, Sched. 1, para. 13, *post,* pp. 67, 155.
[8] *Smalley* v. *Quarrier* [1975] 1 W.L.R. 938, *post,* p. 55.
[9] *Reeves* v. *Davies* [1921] 2 K.B. 486.
[10] *Post,* Chap. 7.
[11] But even if the contractual tenancy did not prohibit sub-letting, a sub-letting of the whole gives rise to a ground for possession under Case 6, *post,* p. 78.
[12] So that the sub-tenant, though subject to Case 6, may have rights under R.A. 1977, s.137, *post,* p. 124.

statutory tenancy to cease, as the tenant can no longer satisfy the residence requirement of section 2.[13]

The Requirement of Occupation as a Residence

As stated above, a statutory tenancy arises on termination of a protected tenancy, so long as the tenant continues to occupy the dwelling-house as his residence. This is so whether the former protected tenancy terminated by expiry, notice to quit,[14] forfeiture,[15] or any other method. As the tenant is entitled by statute to remain in possession, acceptance of rent by the landlord after termination of the protected tenancy will not normally give rise to the inference of a new contractual tenancy.[16]

The occupation must be that of the person who was the protected tenant on termination of the tenancy. So where protected tenancy vests in the trustee in bankruptcy upon the bankruptcy of a protected tenant, no statutory tenancy can arise on termination of the protected tenancy upon disclaimer by the trustee in bankruptcy. This is because the trustee in bankruptcy was the protected tenant immediately before the termination of the tenancy. Continuing occupation by the former protected tenant does not suffice.[17] Nor can a statutory tenancy arise in favour of an occupier whose contractual tenancy was not protected.[18]

The main issue is to define the meaning of the phrase "if and so long as he occupies the dwelling-house as his residence," which is fundamental to the statutory tenancy. The numerous case-law illustrations might best be understood by dividing them into the following categories.

(i) Company and institutional tenants

Such tenants can qualify as protected tenants, and hence enjoy the benefit of rent control.[19] They cannot, however, acquire statu-

---

[13] See *Trustees of Henry Smith's Charity* v. *Willson* [1983] Q.B. 316, *post*, p. 124. It may be otherwise in the case of a short sub-letting, where the tenant intends to return.

[14] But see Case 5, *post*, p. 77, giving a discretionary ground for possession where the *tenant* gives notice to quit and then stays on.

[15] The reason for the forfeiture will normally give rise to a discretionary ground for possession under Case 1 (breach), *post*, p. 74.

[16] *Murray, Bull & Co. Ltd.* v. *Murray* [1953] 1 Q.B. 211.

[17] *Smalley* v. *Quarrier* [1975] 1 W.L.R. 938.

[18] See *Landau* v. *Sloane* [1982] A.C. 490.

[19] *Cf. St. Catherine's College* v. *Dorling* [1980] 1 W.L.R. 66, *ante*, p. 17, where the tenancy was not even protected, as the house was not let as "a" separate dwelling.

tory tenancies, because neither a company nor any other institution is capable of residence.[20] Occupation by servants or agents does not suffice.

Hence the attraction of the common "company let" scheme as a device to avoid security of tenure. If the actual occupant is a licensee, he will have no rights against the landlord. If, on the other hand, he is a lawful sub-tenant, he may have rights not only against the company but also against the head landlord on determination of the company's tenancy.[21]

Although the House of Lords in *Street* v. *Mountford*,[22] in the context of licences, gave the concept of a sham a wider meaning than was perhaps previously thought, it is suggested that there is nothing in that decision to cast doubt upon the efficacy of the "company let" scheme. To regard such a letting as a sham would be to rewrite the company law doctrine of corporate personality. One effect of that decision, however, may be that it will be more difficult to establish that the occupier is in fact the licensee of the company, as opposed to its sub-tenant.

There are, however, certain dicta, although not very persuasive, to the effect that a non-occupying "nominal" tenant might not be recognised if the "real" tenant is known to be someone else. In *Cove* v. *Flick*,[23] where a tenant who rented a home for his family's occupation failed to establish a statutory tenancy, Denning L.J. (as he then was) said "I can well see that the court would not allow a landlord to evade the Act by taking an absent member of the family as nominal tenant when the real occupier and real tenant was to be a present member."[24] Similarly in *S.L. Dando Ltd.* v. *Hitchcock*,[25] where the manager of the tenant company resided. Residence by an agent was held insufficient, otherwise a tenant could get security as to several dwellings. This would be contrary to the purpose of the Rent Act, which is to protect the tenant's enjoyment of his home. But Denning L.J. again said "Let me add a word of caution. I can well see that the court would not allow the landlord to avoid the Acts by taking someone as a nominal tenant,

---

[20] *St. Catherine's College* v. *Dorling, supra*; *Hiller* v. *United Dairies* (*London*) *Ltd.* [1934] 1 K.B. 57. Similarly an individual non-occupying tenant can be protected, but not statutory; *Feather Supplies* v. *Ingham* [1971] 2 Q.B. 348 (father took tenancy for occupation of student son).

[21] R.A. 1977, s.137, *post,* p. 120.

[22] [1985] A.C. 809, *ante,* p. 10. See also the "holiday letting" cases, *ante,* p. 28.

[23] [1954] 2 Q.B. 326n.

[24] *Ibid.* at p. 328.

[25] [1954] 2 Q.B. 317.

well knowing that the real tenant was someone else. The court would then look to the realities of the situation."[26]

There seem to have been no cases where the argument has succeeded. What must be shown is that the agreement is a sham, which is clearly not the case where the tenant company is responsible for the payment of the rent and the performance of the covenants. So in *Firstcross Ltd.* v. *East West (Export/Import) Ltd.*,[27] where a flat was let to a company for its director's occupation, no statutory tenancy could arise. In the absence of any allegation that the agreement was a sham, it could not be claimed that the director was the "real" tenant. Similarly in *Metropolitan Properties Co. Ltd.* v. *Cronan*,[28] where May L.J. said that this

> "apparent exception, if indeed it can ever be made good in law, applies only where the landlord grants the tenancy to the nominal tenant as a sham and for the purpose of being free of the burdens of the Rent Acts to which he would otherwise be subject in respect of the "real" tenant. Where by a genuine transaction, albeit that the true facts are known to the landlord, the latter lets a dwelling-house to one person . . . for the purpose of its occupation by another . . . then when the contractual tenancy expires I do not think that the [occupier] is entitled to the protection of the Rent Acts."[29]

This admittedly gave the landlord the best of both worlds, but he was entitled to make what use he wished of the premises.

In conclusion, where there is a letting to a company (or institution) the consequence is that the company cannot acquire a statutory tenancy, nor can the occupier claim to be the "real" tenant (and, therefore, entitled to a statutory tenancy), unless it can be established that the agreement was a sham. According to the authorities discussed above, this will prove extremely difficult.

(ii) Absentee tenants

"To retain possession or occupation for the purpose of retaining protection the tenant cannot be compelled to spend twenty-four hours in all weathers under his own roof for three hundred and sixty-five days in the year."[30]

---

[26] *Ibid.* at p. 322.
[27] (1981) 41 P. & C.R. 145; [1982] Conv. 151 (J. Martin).
[28] (1982) 44 P. & C.R. 1; [1982] Conv. 384 (J. Martin).
[29] *Ibid.* at p. 9.
[30] *Brown* v. *Brash and Ambrose* [1948] 2 K.B. 247 at 254.

While trivial absences clearly do not break the thread of occupation, the question is to what extent may a more prolonged absence be overlooked. This, as will be seen, is a question of degree, relevant considerations being the length of and reason for the absence, the tenant's intention, and the occupation of the premises during his absence.

The classic case is *Brown* v. *Brash and Ambrose*,[31] where the tenant was absent through imprisonment for two years, leaving his mistress and children in occupation. She subsequently left, taking the children and most of the furniture. Thereafter the tenant's relatives sometimes came in to clean. It was held that the tenant was no longer residing. The fact that his absence was involuntary did not assist him. Clearly temporary absences, for example for holidays, are irrelevant. Nevertheless, as Asquith L.J. explained,

"absence may be sufficiently prolonged or uninterrupted to compel the inference, prima facie, of a cesser of possession or occupation. The question is one of fact and degree. Assume an absence sufficiently prolonged to have this effect: The legal result seems to us to be as follows: (1) The onus is then on the tenant to repel the presumption that his possession has ceased.[32] (2) In order to repel it he must at all events establish a de facto intention on his part to return after his absence. (3) But we are of opinion that neither in principle nor on the authorities can this be enough. To suppose that he can absent himself for five or ten years or more and retain possession and his protected status simply by proving an inward intention to return after so protracted an absence would be to frustrate the spirit and policy of the Acts. . . . (4) Notwithstanding an absence so protracted the authorities suggest that its effect may be averted if he couples and clothes his inward intention with some formal, outward, and visible sign of it; that is, installs in the premises some caretaker or representative, be it a relative or not, with the status of a licensee and with the function of preserving the premises for his own ultimate homecoming. There will then, at all events, be someone to profit by the housing accommodation involved, which will not

---

[31] *Supra.* See also *Poland* v. *Earl Cadogan* [1980] 3 All E.R. 544, holding that the test for residence under the Rent Act is less stringent than that which applies in the context of enfranchisment under the Leasehold Reform Act 1967.

[32] The burden of proving that the tenant has gone out of residence is on the landlord. See further *Roland House Gardens Ltd.* v. *Cravitz* (1974) 29 P. & C.R. 432.

stand empty. It may be that the same result can be secured by leaving on the premises, as a deliberate symbol of continued occupation, furniture, though we are not clear that this was necessary to the decision in *Brown* v. *Draper*.[33] Apart from authority, in principle, possession in fact (for it is with possession in fact and not with possession in law that we are here concerned) requires not merely an '*animus possidendi*' but a '*corpus possessionis*,' namely, some visible state of affairs in which the animus possidendi finds expression. (5) If the caretaker (to use that term for short) leaves or the furniture is removed from the premises, otherwise than quite temporarily, we are of opinion that the protection, artificially prolonged by their presence, ceases, whether the tenant wills or desires such removal or not."[34]

The tenant failed, therefore, because although he had the necessary "*animus possidendi*," there was no sufficient "*corpus possessionis*." The converse was the case in *Colin Smith Music* v. *Ridge*,[35] where a statutory tenant lived with his mistress and children. The tenant left, intending never to return, and surrendered the tenancy to the landlord, who claimed possession. The mistress claimed that the statutory tenancy continued. Her claim failed, the court indicating, however, that the position would have been otherwise if they had married, as a wife can occupy on her husband's behalf.[36]

The statutory tenancy has survived prolonged absences due to ill health,[37] even, it seems, where death terminates the intention to return.[38] Nor was there any loss of the statutory tenancy in *Richards* v. *Green*,[39] where the tenant left to look after his parents, and, after their death, remained in their house in order to sell it. He left his possessions in his flat, to which he intended to return. He was away for two and a half years, and was still away at the trial. The fact that he had inherited the house, worth £90,000, and consequently did not need protection, was irrelevant. In *Atyeo*

---

[33] [1944] K.B. 309. Furniture was regarded as sufficient in *Hoggett* v. *Hoggett* (1980) 39 P. & C.R. 121 and *Gofor Investments Ltd.* v. *Roberts* (1975) 29 P. & C.R. 366.
[34] [1948] 2 K.B. 247 at 254–255.
[35] [1975] 1 W.L.R. 463.
[36] See *infra*.
[37] *Wigley* v. *Leigh* [1950] 2 K.B. 305.
[38] This may be inferred from *Foreman* v. *Beagley* [1969] 1 W.L.R. 1387 *post*, p. 103, where the statutory tenant died in hospital. Her son's claim to succeed to the statutory tenancy failed on the facts.
[39] (1983) 268 E.G. 443.

v. *Fardoe*[40] the statutory tenant wished to move out of his bungalow for the winter because of its poor condition and his wife's preg-
nancy. He arranged for his son to move in, and purported to
transfer the tenancy to him, to be retransferred in the spring. The
tenant left his possessions in the bungalow. It was held that his
statutory tenancy continued. As the purported assignment was a
nullity,[41] it could have no effect in law. A case which perhaps goes
the furthest is *Gofor Investments Ltd.* v. *Roberts*.[42] The tenant
went abroad, intending to return in eight to ten years, after her
children had been educated. Her furniture remained at the property, where family members sometimes stayed. It was held that
such a prolonged absence would not cause the loss of the statutory
tenancy.

Finally, it is not clear whether the statutory tenancy would survive where the tenant intends to return but is debarred from doing
so by an injunction under the Domestic Violence and Matrimonial
Proceedings Act 1976.[43]

(iii) Where the tenant's spouse resides

The general rule, as we have seen, requires an intention to
return on the part of the absent tenant in order to keep the statutory tenancy alive. To this rule there is an important exception,
which is now statutory. The common law principle was that if the
wife of the absent tenant continued in occupation, her occupation
was that of her husband, so that the statutory tenancy survived
even if he did not intend to return.[44] This was a special case, deriving perhaps from the old doctrine that the husband and wife were
one. It may also have been attributable to the husband's duty to
maintain his wife, which explains why the common law principle
did not apply where the wife was the absentee tenant and the husband remained: she had no duty to maintain him. Nor did the principle apply to any other relationships, such as cohabitation outside
marriage.[45] The principle has been extended by statute. The current provision is section 1(6) of the Matrimonial Homes Act 1983,
providing that a spouse's occupation under section 1 of the 1983

---

[40] (1978) 37 P. & C.R. 494.
[41] *Post*, p. 67.
[42] (1975) 29 P. & C.R. 366.
[43] Probably it would, as such injunctions are not usually imposed indefinitely. See (1978) 128 N.L.J. 154 (J. Martin).
[44] See *Wabe* v. *Taylor* [1952] 2 Q.B. 735.
[45] *Colin Smith Music* v. *Ridge, supra.*

Act[46] shall, for the purpose of the Rent Act 1977, be treated as possession by the other spouse. This may be relied on by husbands also, unlike the common law principle. The tenant spouse presumably remains liable under the tenancy, but, by section 1(5), payments by the occupying spouse are as good as if made by the tenant spouse.

In *Hoggett* v. *Hoggett*[47] the husband was a protected tenant. He purported to surrender the tenancy to the landlord.[48] The wife at that time was temporarily at a women's refuge, but intended to return, and had the right to do so under section 1 of the Matrimonial Homes Act (now the Act of 1983). It was held that no surrender by operation of law was possible where the tenant's wife was still occupying. The wife was regarded as occupying, as she satisfied the *Brown* v. *Brash*[49] test. Thus the tenancy continued, and a purported re-letting of the property by the landlord to the husband's mistress gave the latter no rights against the wife.

The position was somewhat different in *Hulme* v. *Langford*,[50] where a protected tenant left his wife and went to live elsewhere. The wife remained, paying rent, until her death in 1982. In 1977 the tenant had requested the landlord to change the rent book so as to make his wife the tenant, but this was never done. In 1978 the tenancy became statutory after service of a notice to quit. Subsequently a fair rent was registered, the wife being named as the tenant. Upon her death the husband resumed possession. The Court of Appeal upheld his claim that he was still the statutory tenant, rejecting the landlord's argument that there had been a surrender and a re-letting to the wife. While such a surrender could occur on a tripartite agreement to re-let to the wife, there was insufficient evidence to support a re-letting here, hence the husband continued as statutory tenant while his wife occupied.

---

[46] Section 1 gives occupation rights to the spouse of a person who is entitled to occupy a dwelling-house by virtue of a beneficial estate or interest or contract or by virtue of any enactment. It was left open in *Hulme* v. *Langford, infra,* whether the equivalent provision in the 1967 Act applied to statutory tenancies, but it seems clearly to do so.

[47] (1980) 39 P. & C.R. 121.

[48] This was not done by deed or writing, so could only be effective in any event as a surrender by operation of law. Presumably a surrender by deed would have ended the protected tenancy, but would not have prejudiced the wife's right to claim that the statutory tenancy survived, relying on M.H.A. 1983, s.1(6).

[49] *Supra.*

[50] (1985) 50 P. & C.R. 199. It was left open whether s.1(5) of the Matrimonial Homes Act 1967 (now the Act of 1983), whereby occupation by the spouse is deemed to be possession by the tenant, would prejudice the establishment of a reletting to the spouse.

However, a spouse can only rely on this principle during the subsistence of the marriage. In *Metropolitan Properties Ltd.* v. *Cronan*[51] the tenant left the property, where his wife and child remained, with no intent to return. The parties were subsequently divorced. The landlord was held entitled to possession, as the wife's protection ceased on the divorce. The wife should have taken steps to secure a transfer of the tenancy upon her divorce.[52] (Under the present law, a transfer order may be made after the decree absolute, but only where the statutory tenancy still exists[53]). The court also rejected the novel proposition that there was a similar exception in favour of the tenant's "abandoned child," who could, it was argued, assert that the statutory tenancy continued where the child occupied, even though the tenant did not intend to return. The duties and relationship between husband and wife are different from those between parent and child. As the argument had not been raised before, it was felt that the rejection of the alleged principle would not cause hardship.

(iv) The "two homes" cases

We have already seen that, in appropriate circumstances, two properties can be regarded as a single home.[54] In such cases a statutory tenancy can clearly arise. The case to be considered here, however, is where the two properties are not let as a single home. The tenant may own one home and rent another, as to which he asserts a statutory tenancy. Or he may rent two homes, and assert a statutory tenancy as to either or both. As will be seen, such claims may succeed, but the first issue is to decide whether it is properly a case of "two homes." In most cases of absence, the tenant will be living elsewhere, but it is not always appropriate to describe the tenant as having two homes. Thus in *Richards* v. *Green*[55] the court declined to regard the tenant as a "two homes man." The rented flat was his sole home, which he continued sufficiently to occupy, hence his statutory tenancy survived. Another example is *Regalian Securities Ltd.* v. *Scheuer.*[56] The statutory tenant of a flat

---

[51] (1982) 44 P. & C.R. 1; [1982] Conv. 384 (J.E.M.).
[52] *Post,* p. 67.
[53] *Lewis* v. *Lewis* [1985] A.C. 828, *post,* p. 68.
[54] *Ante,* p. 17.
[55] (1983) 268 E.G. 443, *supra*; *Heglibiston Establishment* v. *Heyman* (1978) 36 P. & C.R. 351 (statutory tenancy continued although the tenant spent only two or three nights a week at the property, and was often abroad. It was his sole home). See also *Hampstead Way Investments Ltd.* v. *Lewis-Weare, infra.*
[56] (1984) 47 P. & C.R. 367; [1983] Conv. 146 (J.E.M.).

moved into a house bought by his future wife and established a home there. He still used the flat to work in, and kept his clothes and furniture there, and his mail was also sent there. He ate and slept at the house for most of the year. In the winter the house was let and the family stayed elsewhere, "camping" at the flat for about two months a year. It was held that the tenant was no longer entitled to the statutory tenancy of the flat. It was not a "two homes" case, as the house was his only real home. His continuing occupation of the flat did not have the character of residence that is within the contemplation of the Rent Act.

Where, however, the circumstances are such that the tenant can properly be regarded as having two homes, it is established that Rent Act protection may be retained as to either or both.[57] So in *Langford Property Co. Ltd.* v. *Tureman,*[58] where the tenant rented a town flat and owned a country home, he was held entitled to a statutory tenancy of the flat. A *"pied-à-terre,"* however, will not suffice,[59] nor will a "holiday home."[60]

A difficult case is *Kavanagh* v. *Lyroudias,*[61] where a tenant of two adjoining properties was held not to be entitled to a statutory tenancy of one, as he did not occupy it separately from the adjoining premises as a complete home. He was tenant of No. 21, which he shared with a friend, but later took a tenancy of No. 23 as well, from the same landlord, to get an extra bedroom. He slept at No. 23, but ate and used the bathroom at No. 21. He was held to have no statutory tenancy of No. 23, as his occupation of it did not have the character of residence, which requires all the essential activities of living. It seems, however, that his tenancy of No. 23 was initially protected.[62] The House of Lords has subsequently commented[63] that the reasoning of the Court of Appeal in this case was marred by a failure to consider whether the two properties together constituted the tenant's residence.

The House of Lords has recently reviewed the "two homes" principle in *Hampstead Way Investments Ltd.* v. *Lewis-Weare.*[64] A statutory tenant married and moved to a nearby house, retaining his flat, where he slept five times a week after night work. His

---

[57] *Hallwood Estates Ltd.* v. *Flack* [1950] W.N. 268; *Haskins* v. *Lewis* [1931] 2 K.B. 1; *Skinner* v. *Geary* [1931] 2 K.B. 546.
[58] [1949] 1 K.B. 29.
[59] *Beck* v. *Scholz* [1953] 1 Q.B. 570.
[60] *Walker* v. *Ogilvy* (1974) 28 P. & C.R. 288.
[61] [1985] 1 All E.R. 560. Leave was given to appeal to the House of Lords.
[62] Contrast the cases on "dwelling" for the purpose of R.A. 1977, s.1, *ante,* p. 19.
[63] In *Hampstead Way Investments Ltd.* v. *Lewis-Weare, infra.*
[64] [1985] 1 W.L.R. 164.

clothes were kept in the flat, and his mail was sent there; however, he did not eat there. The tenant's stepson lived in the flat, but the tenant paid the outgoings of both properties. The House of Lords held that while it was possible to have two homes within section 2,[65] if one is occupied occasionally or for a limited purpose, it is a question of fact and degree whether the tenant is "residing" there. If the tenant occupied two different parts of the same house under different lettings by the same landlord, carrying on some activities in one part and the rest in the other, he would not be protected as to either part, unless it could be regarded as a single combined letting.[66] If he owns a dwelling-house which he occupies as his home for most of the time, and is tenant of another, which he occupies rarely or for a limited purpose, it is a question of fact and degree whether the second is a home. In the present case the tenant's limited use of the flat was insufficient. It was not his home, but the stepson's. Nor could the house and flat be regarded as one living unit.

This "fact and degree" test has been criticised on the basis that the House of Lords should have taken the opportunity to declare that the policy of the Act is that the tenant should not be protected if the property is not his main residence.[67]

It is interesting to compare the requirements of public sector secure tenancies. By section 81 of the Housing Act 1985, the tenant can only obtain protection as to his only or principal home. No doubt the possibility of the "two homes man" was not present to the minds of the drafters of the original Rent Act legislation, which was designed for the poorer classes. Subsequent experience has indicated the need for a specific provision in the Housing Act. A similar provision would be welcome in the Rent Act.

Finally, it might be added that a lenient interpretation of section 2, in particular the "two homes" cases and those involving lengthy absences, has repercussions on the resident landlord rule, discussed in Chapter 3. In order to satisfy that rule, and thereby deprive the tenant of full protection, the landlord must occupy part of the same building as his residence.[68] This requires him to fulfil the same conditions as a statutory tenant must fulfil under section 2.[69] Hence the *Brown* v. *Brash*[70] test is imported here, with the result that landlords can presumably rely on the cases which

---

[65] Confirming *Langford Property Co. Ltd.* v. *Tureman, supra.*
[66] *Wimbush* v. *Cibulia* [1949] 2 K.B. 564, *ante*, p. 24.
[67] [1985] Conv. 224 (P. F. Smith).
[68] R.A. 1977, s.12.
[69] *Ibid.* Sched. 2, para. 5.
[70] *Supra.*

were decided on the basis of furthering the policy of the Rent Act to protect the tenant. Perhaps a stricter approach might be expected, but there is, as yet, no authority on the point.

(v) Joint tenants

The Rent Act makes no express provision for joint tenancies.[71] On a literal reading of section 2 in the case of a joint protected tenancy, the statutory tenancy can only arise if both tenants continue to reside, as they together constitute the tenant. The matter arose in *Lloyd* v. *Sadler*,[72] where one joint tenant left while the tenancy was still protected. The other remained, and subsequently claimed a statutory tenancy. The Court of Appeal, rejecting the literal approach, upheld the tenant's claim. As the policy of the Act was to protect the tenant, the Act should be construed in his favour. The strict law of joint tenancy did not apply. It was argued that this result would prejudice the landlord, who, during the protected tenancy, had been able to look to both tenants for the rent. However, if the rent was not paid, there would be a ground for possession.[73] In any case, if one joint tenant had died during the protected tenancy, the other would have become sole tenant (and subsequently sole statutory tenant) by survivorship. No doubt if both had remained, they would have become joint statutory tenants.

However, certain problems remain to be resolved. Assuming both became joint statutory tenants, how do the rules relating to statutory tenants by succession[74] apply on the death of one joint tenant? Must the claimant be a member of the family of both? Does he take jointly with the survivor? Indeed it may be doubted whether the successor rules apply at all. These matters are further discussed in Chapter 7.

Terms of the Statutory Tenancy

Section 3(1) of the 1977 Act provides that the statutory tenant, so long as he retains possession, "shall observe and be entitled to the benefit of all the terms and conditions of the original contract of

---

[71] See generally [1978] Conv. 436 (J. Martin), comparing other statutory codes.
[72] [1978] Q.B. 774.
[73] Under Case 1, *post*, p. 74.
[74] *Post*, Chap. 7.

tenancy, so far as they are consistent with the provisions of this Act." As a general rule, therefore, the type of covenants which are regarded as "touching and concerning" the land at common law, such as the covenant to repair or the covenant for quiet enjoyment, will continue into the statutory tenancy. Section 3(2) expressly provides that the statutory tenant shall afford the landlord access and reasonable facilities for executing repairs which the landlord is entitled to execute.[75]

Terms which have been regarded as inconsistent include, obviously, the covenant to yield up possession at the end of the tenancy,[76] and also an option to purchase the reversion "at any time" at a fixed price.[77]

The Act makes express provision as to the terms of the statutory tenancy in three further respects.

(i) Rent

The rent payable under the statutory tenancy is not necessarily the same as that payable under the previous protected tenancy. This is discussed in Chapter 10.

(ii) Notice

By section 3(3), a statutory tenant shall be entitled to give up possession only if he gives such notice as would have been required under the protected tenancy (*i.e.* if periodic), or, if no notice would have been required (*i.e.* if fixed term), on giving not less than three months notice. By the Protection from Eviction Act 1977, section 5,[78] a minimum of four weeks notice is required for a periodic tenancy. A landlord who obtains a possession order against a statutory tenant is not required to give notice to quit, even though such a notice would have been required during the protected tenancy.[79]

The statutory tenant may ask or receive payment from the landlord as a condition of giving up possession, but commits an offence if he asks or receives payment from any other person.[80]

---

[75] See also s.148, implying a similar term into protected tenancies.
[76] *Barton* v. *Fincham* [1921] 2 K.B. 291.
[77] *Longmuir* v. *Kew* [1960] 1 W.L.R. 862. The option was exercisable only during the contractual tenancy. *Cf. William McIlroy Ltd.* v. *Clements* [1923] W.N. 81 (option to renew).
[78] *Ante*, p. 8.
[79] R.A. 1977, s.3(4).
[80] *Ibid.*, Sched. 1, para. 12. Note that a purchaser does not become landlord until completion.

We have seen that, according to the case-law discussed in this chapter, the statutory tenancy ceases if the tenant goes out of residence. What, then, is the position if he loses his statutory tenancy but has not given the notice to quit required by section 3? It seems that while such a tenant loses his rights to a statutory tenancy, he continues to be liable to pay the rent until such a notice is served, unless there is surrender and acceptance.[81] It was left open by the House of Lords in *Lewis* v. *Lewis*[82] whether in such a case the tenancy would be regarded as subsisting for the purpose of a transfer order to the tenant's divorced wife.

(iii) Assignment

The prior protected tenancy will have been assignable unless it contained a covenant to the contrary. The statutory tenancy, on the other hand, is not capable of assignment. Any purported assignment of it is a nullity, although if the statutory tenant ceases to reside, the statutory tenancy will normally terminate.[83] If the protected tenancy contained no prohibition against sub-letting, the statutory tenant may sub-let. If, however, he sub-lets the whole, the statutory tenancy will cease, as the tenant will have ceased to reside.[84]

There are two exceptions to the rule that the statutory tenancy may not be assigned.

(a) Where the landlord is a party

Where there is a written agreement, to which the landlord is a party, the statutory tenant may give up possession in favour of a third party, who is thereafter deemed to be the statutory tenant.[85]

(b) By court order in matrimonial proceedings[86]

By section 7 of the Matrimonial Homes Act 1967, the court was empowered to order the transfer of a statutory (or protected) tenancy on divorce or annulment. Such an order could not be

---

[81] See *Boyer* v. *Warbey* [1953] 1 Q.B. 234; *King's College, Cambridge* v. *Kershman* (1948) 64 T.L.R. 547. It is arguable that the personal representative of a deceased statutory tenant must, in cases where there is no successor, give notice to quit to the landlord.

[82] [1985] A.C. 828; *infra.*

[83] See *Atyeo* v. *Fardoe* (1978) 37 P. & C.R. 494, *ante,* p. 59. Contrast the position at common law, where a tenancy may be effectively assigned, although in breach of covenant.

[84] *Post,* p. 124. See also Case 6, *post,* p. 77.

[85] R.A. 1977, Sched. 1, para. 13.

[86] See [1982] Conv. 334 (A. Arden).

made after decree absolute. This power was extended by the Matrimonial Homes and Property Act 1981, so that a transfer order could be made on the granting of a decree of divorce, nullity or judicial separation, "or at any time thereafter." Thus the power continues exercisable after decree absolute. This provision is now contained in Schedule 1, paragraph 1, of the consolidating Matrimonial Homes Act 1983. It has since been enacted that the transfer order may be made without any decree of divorce, nullity, etc., where an application is made by a party to a marriage for an order for financial relief.[87]

The question which arose in *Lewis* v. *Lewis*[88] was whether the provision in the 1981 Act, giving the court jurisdiction after decree absolute, was retrospective. The parties were divorced before the provision was in operation. The House of Lords held that it was not retrospective. Even if it had been, it would not have availed the wife, as the statutory tenancy came to an end on decree absolute.[89] Where the statutory tenant no longer resides, his spouse's occupation will only keep the statutory tenancy alive until decree absolute.[90] The statutory provisions relating to transfer orders use the present tense: "Where one spouse is entitled . . . to occupy a dwelling-house by virtue of a protected tenancy or statutory tenancy. . . . "[91] Hence the court has no jurisdiction where the statutory tenancy has already terminated. This result is not only clearly correct but also, it is submitted, desirable. It would be unfair to the landlord to resurrect a statutory tenancy which has ceased to exist.

It remains to consider the circumstances in which a transfer order can be made after decree absolute. This can clearly be done if the tenancy is still protected, as occupation by the tenant is not there required. Where the tenancy is statutory, it will only continue after decree absolute if the tenant himself remains in occupation. In such a case the spouse may apply for a transfer order, whether occupying with the tenant spouse or non-occupying. If the tenant is not in occupation, the spouse must apply before decree absolute.

---

[87] Matrimonial and Family Proceedings Act 1984, s.22.

[88] [1985] A.C. 828; [1985] Conv. 128 (J.E.M.).

[89] See *Metropolitan Properties Ltd.* v. *Cronan* (1982) 44 P. & C.R. 1, *ante,* p. 62.

[90] M.H.A. 1983, s.1(6), re-enacting similar provisions in the previous legislation.

[91] M.H.A. 1983, Sched. 1, para. 1.

Chapter 6

RECOVERY OF POSSESSION

A statutory tenancy terminates if one of the following four events occurs[1]: the tenant yields up possession after giving proper notice (as discussed in Chapter 5); the tenant dies without leaving a successor to the statutory tenancy (to be discussed in Chapter 7); the landlord obtains a court order based on one of the grounds for possession in the Rent Act 1977; or some other event occurs such as a change of user or transfer of the reversion to a person not bound by the Act, whereupon the tenant ceases to be entitled to retain possession as statutory (or protected) tenant.

Two things should be noted about the statutory grounds for possession. First, some are discretionary, so that the court will only grant possession if it considers it reasonable to do so, while others are mandatory. Secondly, if the tenancy is still protected (as opposed to statutory), the landlord must be able to terminate it under the general law, for example, by forfeiture or notice to quit, in addition to establishing a statutory ground for possession. If the tenancy is already statutory, the landlord can go straight to the grounds for possession, as the common law methods of termination no longer apply.

Before examining the grounds for possession, the effect of over-crowding should be mentioned. Section 101 of the Rent Act 1977 provides that at any time when a dwelling-house is overcrowded, within the meaning of the Housing Act 1985, in such circumstances as to render the occupier guilty of an offence, nothing in Part VII of the Act (dealing with recovery of possession from protected or statutory tenants and from occupiers holding under restricted contracts) shall prevent the immediate landlord of the occupier from obtaining possession. A former restriction whereby the section's application was confined to premises used "by members of the working classes or of a type suitable for such use" was finally repealed in 1985.[2]

---

[1] If wrongfully evicted, the statutory tenant may obtain damages for trespass (see *Drane* v. *Evangelou* [1978] 1 W.L.R. 455, *ante*, p. 6). If unable to obtain an injunction in time to restrain a trespass or unlawful eviction, he may obtain a mandatory injunction to restore him to possession.

[2] Housing (Consequential Provisions) Act 1985, Sched. 2.

The effect of section 101 is to deprive the tenant of his security while the overcrowding lasts, but rent control still applies prior to the making of a possession order. Of course, section 101 does not enable the landlord to recover possession against a protected tenant unless he is in a position to terminate the contractual tenancy.

If the overcrowding has ceased before the hearing, the landlord will be unable to recover possession.[3] Nor may he do so if the local authority has licensed the overcrowding, as the occupier then commits no offence.[4]

Although not specifically dealt with in the 1977 Act, a similar principle applies to unfit houses.[5]

Suitable Alternative Accommodation

This is dealt with under a separate heading because, although in effect a ground for possession, it does not appear in the statutory list of grounds for possession, discussed below.

By section 98 of the 1977 Act, the court may make an order for possession if it is satisfied that suitable alternative accommodation is available for the tenant (or will be available for him when the order takes effect). Such an order will not be made unless the court considers it reasonable to make it. Whether the alternative accommodation is suitable depends on the extent to which the statutory criteria are fulfilled.[6] The alternative accommodation need not be offered by the landlord himself. A local authority certificate to the effect that the authority will provide suitable alternative accommodation for the tenant in the district by a specified date is conclusive evidence as to the availability of suitable alternative accommodation. Failing such a certificate, accommodation is deemed suitable if it satisfies two broad requirements: first as to security of tenure, and secondly as to its suitability to the particular circumstances of the tenant. As far as security is concerned, the alternative accommodation must be premises let as a separate dwelling in such manner that there will be either a protected tenancy (other than one to which any of the mandatory grounds for possession, discussed below, will apply[7]) or on terms which will

---

[3] *Zbytniewski* v. *Broughton* [1956] 2 Q.B. 673.
[4] H.A. 1985, s.327. Nor is the offence committed where the overcrowding occurs solely by reason of a child attaining a specified age, if the tenant has applied to the local authority for alternative accommodation; *ibid.*, s.328.
[5] See *Buswell* v. *Goodwin* [1971] 1 W.L.R. 92, *post*, p. 91.
[6] Set out in R.A. 1977, Sched. 15, paras. 3–8.
[7] H.A. 1980, Sched. 25, para. 58. A shorthold tenancy is, therefore, not suitable.

afford security reasonably equivalent to such a protected tenancy. "Reasonably equivalent" security will be provided by a local authority secure tenancy, or by a long fixed term letting,[8] but not by a letting which creates only a restricted contract.

As far as the particular tenant's requirements are concerned, the alternative accommodation must be reasonably suitable to the needs of the tenant and his family with regard to proximity to work, to the means of the tenant, and to the needs of the tenant and his family as regards extent and character.[9] If the current tenancy is furnished, so must the proposed tenancy of the alternative accommodation be.

Naturally the statutory criteria outlined above cannot deal with every circumstance, hence there is much case-law on the meaning of suitable alternative accommodation. The question whether the alternative accommodation is suitable must be kept distinct from the question whether, even though suitable, it is reasonable to make the possession order. In *Battlespring* v. *Gates*[10] an elderly widow was offered a similar, but more pleasant and comfortable flat. This was suitable alternative accommodation, but it was not reasonable to make the order, because the widow has lived there for 35 years and was attached to her flat and its memories. The question of reasonableness is for the judge in the first instance, whose finding will not be upset on appeal unless he has misdirected himself. It involves a consideration of both landlord and tenant. Here the landlord's interest in recovering possession was purely financial. There was nothing wrong in that, but the position was different from that of a landlord who wished to recover possession because he had nowhere to live himself.

As we have seen, the needs not only of the tenant but also of his "family" must be taken into account. It was held in *Kavanagh* v. *Lyroudias*[11] that the word bears the same meaning as it does in the context of succession to the statutory tenancy.[12] In that case the

---

[8] See county court cases discussed in Pettit, *Private Sector Tenancies* (2nd ed.), p. 193.
[9] As to means and needs, it suffices to show that, as regards rental and extent, the accommodation is similar to that provided by the local authority in the neighbourhood for persons with similar needs as regards extent; R.A. 1977, Sched. 15, para. 5(1)(*a*). See also para. 5(2), as to evidence.
[10] (1983) 268 E.G. 355. See also *Gladyric Ltd.* v. *Collinson* (1983) 267 E.G. 761 (understanding that property to be let for a short time only held relevant to reasonableness).
[11] [1985] 1 All E.R. 560. See also *Standingford* v. *Probert* [1950] 1 K.B. 377.
[12] *Post*, Chap. 7.

tenant shared his home with a sick friend. The friend was held not to be "family," hence his needs were not relevant to the suitability of any alternative accommodation. However, it would not be reasonable to make a possession order where the alternative accommodation would be such that the tenant would have to share a cramped flat with the friend or eject him.

The question whether the alternative accommodation is suitable to the tenant's "needs" as regards extent and character requires a consideration of his *housing* needs. In *Hill* v. *Rochard*[13] the tenants occupied a large period country house with grounds and a paddock for their pony. The landlord offered a modern detached house with no paddock on an estate outside a village. This was held to be suitable alternative accommodation. The present tenancy allowed the tenants to enjoy amenities far beyond their housing needs, but the Rent Act was not concerned with matters such as proximity to entertainment, recreation and sport.

Environmental matters, however, are relevant. In *Redspring* v. *Francis*[14] the tenant had lived for 30 years in a small flat in a quiet residential road. The tenant had the use of a garden, but the bathroom was shared. The landlord offered a flat with larger rooms and an exclusive bathroom, but no garden. This flat was in a busy road, next door to a fried fish shop, and near to a hospital, cinema and public house. In addition, the local authoriity planned to use a yard at the back as a transport depot. The Court of Appeal, finding that this was not suitable alternative accommodation, held that the environment could be considered, as well as the physical character of the property. Here the difference was in kind and not merely of degree.

This case was distinguished by the Court of Appeal in *Siddiqui* v. *Rashid*,[15] where the tenant, a Muslim, had a flat in London and worked in Luton. His friends were all in London, where he attended a mosque and a cultural centre. The offer of a flat in Luton was held suitable. While the court could consider the environment, it need not consider the society of friends, nor the tenant's cultural or spiritual interests.

It is established that a part of the property which is the subject-

---

[13] [1983] 1 W.L.R. 478; [1983] Conv. 320 (P. F. Smith). See also, in the context of public sector secure tenancies, *Enfield London Borough Council* v. *French* (1985) 49 P. & C.R. 223, where the need for a garden as a hobby was a "need" within the statute, although on the facts it was outweighed by other considerations.
[14] [1973] 1 W.L.R. 134.
[15] [1980] 1 W.L.R. 1018.

matter of the current letting can constitute alternative accommodation. In *Mykolyshyn* v. *Noah*[16] the letting comprised a bedroom, kitchen and sitting-room. The sitting-room was used only to store furniture. The landlord, wishing to take it over as a bedroom for his children, offered the same flat minus the sitting-room. This was held to be suitable alternative accommodation.

This principle is useful where the tenant has sublet part of the property. The landlord can effectively take over the sublet part[17] by offering the tenant the remainder. The policy of the Rent Act is to protect the tenant in his home, and not to let him profit from his security by subletting. However, there is no hard and fast rule. So in *Yoland Ltd.* v. *Reddington*,[18] where the tenant had sublet part to friends (who shared the bathroom and garden), an offer of the remainder was held suitable, but nevertheless it was not reasonable to make the order. The tenant would no longer be surrounded by sub-tenants of his own choosing and the landlord (an investment company which had purchased the reversion) might leave the other part empty and uncared for.

The Discretionary Grounds for Possession

The various "Cases" giving rise to a ground for possession are set out in Schedule 15 of the 1977 Act. Part I of that Schedule contains ten "Cases" which are discretionary. The court must consider it reasonable to make such an order.[19]

We have already seen, in the context of suitable alternative accommodation, some of the factors which have been relevant to the exercise of the discretion. It does not follow from the fact the landlord is being reasonable in requiring possession that it is reasonable to order possession: "because a wish is reasonable, it does not follow that it is reasonable in a court to grant it."[20] The

---

[16] [1970] 1 W.L.R. 1271. See also *McDonnell* v. *Daly* [1969] 1 W.L.R. 1482, holding (at a time when dwellings with a partial business use could be within the Rent Act) that an offer of a part of the same dwelling could not be suitable alternative accommodation when the "subtracted" part (an artist's studio) was necessary to the tenant's professional needs.

[17] For the sub-tenant's position, see R.A. 1977, s.137, *post*, p. 120.

[18] (1982) 263 E.G. 157.

[19] R.A. 1977, s.98(1).

[20] *Shrimpton* v. *Rabbits* (1924) 131 L.T. 478 at 479, in the context of Case 9, *infra*.

general principle has been stated by Lord Greene M.R. in *Cumming* v. *Danson*[21]: the judge must consider

> "all relevant circumstances as they exist at the date of the hearing. That he must do in what I venture to call a broad, common-sense way as a man of the world, and come to the conclusion giving such weight as he thinks right to the various factors in the situation. Some factors may have little or no weight, others may be decisive, but it is quite wrong for him to exclude from his consideration matters which he ought to take into account."

The issue of reasonableness is for the county court judge to decide. The Court of Appeal will not interfere with the exercise of his discretion unless he has erred in law.

It is now proposed to consider in turn the various discretionary grounds for possession.

Case 1

> "Where any rent lawfully due from the tenant has not been paid or any obligation of the protected or statutory tenancy . . . has been broken or not performed."

This ground is primarily concerned with a tenant who has a "bad record."[22] The landlord is unlikely to recover possession in the case of an isolated breach. The commencement of proceedings is the date at which the breach must exist, but possession is unlikely to be ordered where the tenant has paid arrears before judgment, unless there is a long history of arrears.[23] In any event, the court has a discretion to suspend the operation of a possession order on conditions, for example as to the payment of arrears.[24] Indeed, this is the the the common practice.

---

[21] [1942] 2 All E.R. 653, at 655. See also *Cresswell* v. *Hodgson* [1951] 2 K.B. 92, where Denning L.J. said (at p. 97) that the possession order must be "reasonable having regard to the interests of the parties concerned and also reasonable having regard to the interests of the public." In *Chiverton* v. *Ede* [1921] 2 K.B. 30, at 44–45, McCardie J. said that the discretion must be exercised "in a judicial manner, having regard on the one hand to the general scheme and purpose of the Act, and on the other to the special conditions, including to a large extent matters of a domestic and social character."

[22] *Dellenty* v. *Pellow* [1951] 2 K.B. 858.

[23] The Common Law Procedure Act 1852, s.212, does not, however, apply to a statutory tenant; *Dellenty* v. *Pellow*, *supra*. See generally *Bird* v. *Hildage* [1948] 1 K.B. 91; *Hayman* v. *Rowlands* [1957] 1 W.L.R. 317.

[24] R.A. 1977, s.100, *post*, p. 90.

As far as breaches other than non-payment of rent are concerned, Case 1 applies to express and implied obligations, whether or not continuing.[25] If the breach has been remedied, however, this will be significant to the issue of reasonableness.[26]

The common law doctrine of waiver is not fully applicable to statutory tenancies, hence acceptance of rent in the knowledge of a breach will not inevitably preclude the landlord from invoking Case 1,[27] even if the acceptance is unqualified.[28] This is because waiver relates strictly to forfeiture, which is not applicable to a statutory tenancy.[29]

Case 2

> "Where the tenant or any person residing or lodging with him or any sub-tenant of his has been guilty of conduct which is a nuisance or annoyance to adjoining occupiers, or has been convicted of using the dwelling-house or allowing the dwelling-house to be used for immoral or illegal purposes."

"Annoyance" is wider than "nuisance," and has been described as something which "reasonably troubles the mind and pleasure, not of a fanciful person . . . but of the ordinary sensible English inhabitant of a house."[30] Possession may be ordered in respect of a nuisance which has abated, if there is a likelihood that it will arise again.[31]

Occupiers may be "adjoining" even though their premises are not physically adjacent, provided they are near enough to be affected.[32]

Where possession is sought on the basis of a conviction for immoral or illegal user, the conviction must relate to the premises. As Scrutton L.J. has said, "it is enough if there is a conviction of a crime which has been committed on the premises and for the purpose of committing which the premises have been used; but it is

---

[25] For a recent example, see *Florent* v. *Horez* (1984) 48 P. & C.R. 166 (breach of covenant against business user).
[26] *Brown* v. *Davies* [1958] 1 Q.B. 117.
[27] *Oak Property Co. Ltd.* v. *Chapman* [1947] K.B. 886 (where the acceptance was qualified).
[28] *Trustees of Henry Smith's Charity* v. *Willson* [1983] Q.B. 316; *cf. Carter* v. *Green* [1950] 2 K.B. 76.
[29] Although it will, of course, apply if the tenancy is still protected.
[30] *Tod-Heatley* v. *Benham* (1888) 40 Ch.D. 80 at 98.
[31] *Florent* v. *Horez* (1984) 48 P. & C.R. 166 (activities of Turkish Cypriot organization on the premises).
[32] *Cobstone Investments Ltd.* v. *Maxim* [1984] 3 W.L.R. 606; [1985] Conv. 168 (T. J. Lyons).

not enough that the tenant has been convicted of a crime with which the premises have nothing to do beyond merely being the scene of its commission."[33] In *Abrahams* v. *Wilson*[34] the tenant had been convicted of possession of drugs. It was said that if the drugs were merely found in the tenant's pocket or handbag, this would not amount to using the premises, in contrast to the case where the premises were used for storage or as a hiding-place. Even if the tenant had used the premises, possession was not ordered. Although in most such cases it will be considered reasonable to grant possession, here the discretion was exercised in favour of the tenant, because she was unable to work and had a child to support, hence she would suffer hardship if evicted.

Case 3

"Where the condition of the dwelling-house has, in the opinion of the court, deteriorated owing to acts of waste by, or the neglect or default of, the tenant or any person residing or lodging with him or any sub-tenant of his . . . where the court is satisfied that the tenant has not, before the making of the order in question, taken such steps as he ought reasonably to have taken for the removal of the lodger or sub-tenant, as the case may be."

Case 3 can apply even if there is no breach of any obligation of the tenancy.[35] A recent example is *Holloway* v. *Povey*,[36] where the garden of a cottage was seriously neglected. The "dwelling-house," as is apparent from section 26,[37] includes the garden. The possession order was suspended for a year, on condition that the tenant tidied the garden and kept it tidy for that time. A further point was that the tenant, who had succeeded to the statutory tenancy on his mother's death, could not be held responsible for any neglect prior to his mother's death.

Case 4

"Where the condition of any furniture provided for use under the tenancy has, in the opinion of the court, deteriorated owing to ill-treatment by the tenant or any person residing or lodging with him or any sub-tenant of his . . . where the court

[33] *S.Schneider & Sons* v. *Abrahams* [1925] 1 K.B. 301 at 310.
[34] [1971] 2 Q.B. 88.
[35] *Lowe* v. *Lendrum* (1950) 159 E.G. 423.
[36] (1984) 271 E.G. 195.
[37] *Ante*, p. 20.

is satisfied that the tenant has not, before the making of the order in question, taken such steps as he ought reasonably have taken for the removal of the lodger or sub-tenant, as the case may be."

This ground was introduced by the Rent Act 1974, which brought furnished tenancies into full protection.

Case 5

"Where the tenant has given notice to quit and, in consequence of that notice, the landlord has contracted to sell or let the dwelling-house or has taken any other steps as the result of which he would, in the opinion of the court, be seriously prejudiced if he could not obtain possession."

This deals with the situation where the tenant changes his mind after giving notice. The notice to quit must be valid[38]; a mere agreement to surrender will not suffice.[39]

The landlord cannot invoke Case 5 if he merely intends to sell.[40]

Case 6

"Where, without the consent of the landlord, the tenant has[41] . . . assigned or sublet the whole of the dwelling-house or sublet part of the dwelling-house, the remainder being already sublet."

The purpose of this ground, it has been said, is "to give some protection to a landlord against the risk of finding some person wholly unknown to him irrevocably installed in his property."[42]

A statutory tenancy, as we have seen,[43] is incapable of assignment. It has been suggested that this ground originated at a time when it had not been established that a statutory tenancy could not be assigned and when the rules as to the requirement of residence for statutory tenants had not been fully developed.[44] Even though a statutory tenant may sublet, a subletting of the whole will normally terminate the statutory tenancy in any event, as the tenant

---

[38] *De Vries* v. *Sparks* (1927) 137 L.T. 441.
[39] *Standingford* v. *Bruce* [1926] 1 K.B. 466.
[40] *Barton* v. *Fincham* [1921] 2 K.B. 291.
[41] Since certain dates specified in paragraphs (b) to (d).
[42] *Hyde* v. *Pimley* [1952] 2 Q.B. 506 at 512.
[43] *Ante*, p. 67. It is not clear whether Case 6 applies to a purported assignment.
[44] Yates and Hawkins, *Landlord and Tenant Law*, pp. 338–339.

will have ceased to reside. In such circumstances the main reason
for invoking Case 6 will be to recover possession against the sub-
tenant, as explained below.

Case 6 applies even if the subletting is not in breach of any obligation in the tenancy,[45] although the absence of any breach will be
relevant to the exercise of the discretion.[46]

"Consent" need not be written, and may be implied. It suffices
that it was given at any time before commencement of the proceedings.[47] It is doubtful whether mere waiver constitutes consent.[48]

The significance of Case 6 cannot be fully appreciated without a
consideration of the rights of the sub-tenant. This will be fully discussed in Chapter 9. For present purposes, it must suffice to
explain that a lawful sub-tenant may have rights against the head
landlord under section 137 of the 1977 Act. In the case of a subletting in breach of covenant, therefore, there will be a discretionary
ground for possession against the tenant, and the sub-tenant will
have no rights under section 137. Where the subletting is not
unlawful, we have seen that Case 6 nevertheless applies to terminate the tenancy. In such a case the sub-tenant may invoke the protection of section 137, but it has been held that Case 6 is also
available against him in these circumstances.[49] The issue of
reasonableness must, however, be decided as between the landlord and the sub-tenant.

[Case 7, relating to controlled tenancies, was repealed by the
Housing Act, 1980].

Case 8

"Where the dwelling-house is reasonably required by the
landlord for occupation[50] as a residence for some person

---

[45] If it is in breach, Case 1 will also apply.

[46] See *Leith Properties Ltd.* v. *Byrne* [1983] Q.B. 433; [1983] Conv. 155
(J. Martin); *Trustees of Henry Smith's Charity* v. *Willson* [1983] Q.B.
316; [1983] Conv. 248 (J. Martin); *Pazgate Ltd.* v. *McGrath* (1984) 272
E.G. 1069.

[47] *Hyde* v. *Pimley* [1952] 2 Q.B. 506. See also *Regional Properties Co.
Ltd.* v. *Frankenschwerth* [1951] 1 K.B. 631.

[48] Otherwise a tenant who had sublet in breach of covenant would be
better off than a tenant whose subletting was not a breach. See [1983]
Conv. 248 at 252. (J. Martin); *cf.* Pettit, *Private Sector Tenancies* (2nd
ed.) at 204.

[49] *Leith Properties Ltd.* v. *Byrne, supra*; *Trustees of Henry Smith's Charity*
v. *Willson, supra*.

[50] Not necessarily under a tenancy. See generally *R. F. Fuggle* v. *Gadsden*
[1948] 2 K.B. 236.

engaged in his wholetime employment . . . and the tenant[51] was in the employment of the landlord or a former landlord, and the dwelling-house was let to him in consequence of that employment and he has ceased to be in that employment."

If a possession order is granted, but it subsequently appears that it was obtained by misrepresentation or concealment of material facts, section 102 gives the court power to order the landlord to compensate the tenant.

In the case of joint landlords, it presumably suffices that only one of them was the employer of the original tenant and of the proposed new occupier.[52]

Case 9

"Where the dwelling-house is reasonably required by the landlord for occupation as a residence[53] for—

    (a) himself,[54] or
    (b) any son or daughter of his over 18 years of age, or
    (c) his father or mother, or
    (d) the father or mother of his wife or husband,

and the landlord did not become landlord by purchasing the dwelling-house or any interest therein."[55]

It is further provided that the court shall not make a possession order if satisfied that, having regard to all the circumstances, including the question whether other accommodation is available for the landlord or the tenant, greater hardship would be caused by granting the order than by refusing to grant it.[56]

As with Case 8, the court may order compensation under section 102 in cases of misrepresentation or concealment.

---

[51] This means the original tenant. Case 8 is, therefore, available against any statutory tenant by sucession on his death; *Bolsover Colliery Co. Ltd.* v. *Abbott* [1946] K.B. 8.

[52] By analogy with *Tilling* v. *Whiteman* [1980] A.C. 1 *post*, p. 84. It has, however, been held that the Case does not apply where the landlord is not the sole employer; *Grimond* v. *Duncan* (1949) S.C. 195 (employment by partnership including the landlord). *cf.* Case 9, *infra*.

[53] Occupation with a view to sale does not suffice; *Rowe* v. *Truelove* (1976) 241 E.G. 533.

[54] This includes all "normal emanations" of himself, such as his wife or children under 18; *Ritcher* v. *Wilson* [1963] 2 Q.B. 426.

[55] After certain dates specified in paragraphs (i) to (iv).

[56] R.A. 1977, Sched. 15, Part III, para. 1.

Whether the house is "reasonably" required is a separate issue from the question whether it is "reasonable" to make the order.[57]

Although the onus of proving that the dwelling is "reasonably required" is on the landlord, the onus of proving greater hardship is on the tenant.[58]

The "landlord by purchase" restriction is to prevent a sitting tenant from being evicted by a purchaser who has bought the property subject to his tenancy. Clearly the original landlord is not a landlord by purchase; nor is a person who acquired the reversion by will. "Purchase" bears its common meaning of commercial acquisition for money or money's worth. In *Thomas* v. *Fryer*[59] the landlord left the property by will to his four children. One daughter bought out the shares of the others. She was held not to have become landlord by purchase, but by a domestic arrangement.

Normally personal representatives, although clearly "landlords," cannot invoke Case 9, either for their own benefit (because their occupation would be a breach of trust if they have no beneficial interest), or for the benefit of a beneficiary.[60] In exceptional cases, however, they may succeed, as in *Patel* v. *Patel*,[61] where the personal representatives were trustees for the deceased landlord's children. As they had adopted the children and planned to live in the house with them, there was no breach of trust.

Another question is whether the landlord must have an immediate need for the property. The relevant time for establishing that he reasonably requires the property is the date of the hearing.[62] A prior need which no longer exists is insufficient, but what of a future need? In *Kidder* v. *Birch*[63] the plaintiff and her elderly mother owned a small cottage which had been let to the tenants since 1948, and lived themselves in a rented house, which would be too large and expensive to run after the mother's death, which had not yet occurred. A possession order was granted, but suspended

---

[57] *Shrimpton* v. *Rabbits* (1924) 131 L.T. 478, *ante*, p. 73.
[58] *Sims* v. *Wilson* [1946] 2 All E.R. 261; *Manaton* v. *Edwards* (1985) 276 E.G. 1256.
[59] [1970] 1 W.L.R. 845. See also *Littlechild* v. *Holt* [1950] 1 K.B. 1 (person acquiring reversion from a person who became landlord by purchase cannot be in any better position).
[60] *Parker* v. *Rosenberg* [1947] K.B. 371.
[61] [1981] 1 W.L.R. 1342; [1982] Conv. 443 (J.E.M.).
[62] *Alexander* v. *Mohamadzadeh* (1986) 51 P. & C.R. 41. The date of the proceedings, however, is the relevant date for Case 1; *Bird* v. *Hildage* [1948] 1 K.B. 91.
[63] (1983) 265 E.G. 773; [1982] Conv. 444 (J.E.M.).

until the mother's death. On appeal, it was held that the landlord must show a need in the ascertainable and not too distant future. The possession order was varied so that it could be executed if the mother's death should occur within 12 months. If it did not occur within that period, the order should not be executed at all. No doubt this principle is equally applicable to other grounds where the landlord must show that he requires the property for some purpose.

As far as the question of greater hardship is concerned, the court should consider all who may be affected—"relatives, dependants, lodgers, guests, and the stranger within the gates—but should weigh such hardship with due regard to the status of the persons affected, and their 'proximity' to the tenant or landlord, and the extent to which, consequently, hardship to them would be hardship to him."[64] In *Thomas* v. *Fryer*[65] the landlord succeeded when evidence established that her mental health would deteriorate if she did not recover possession.

It has been held that Case 9 cannot be invoked by joint landlords unless both wish to occupy.[66] The matter was left open in the House of Lords in *Tilling* v *Whiteman*,[67] where a contrary view was taken of Case 11 (discussed below). If it is correct that one of joint landlords cannot invoke Case 9, then it follows that joint landlords cannot seek possession of the property as a residence for a son or daughter over 18 unless they are both the child's parents; they cannot seek possession of the property as a residence for a parent unless they are siblings; and they cannot seek possession of the property as a residence for a parent-in-law at all.[68] The difficulties inherent in the narrow construction of "landlord" perhaps indicate that a wider construction might be appropriate.

---

[64] *Harte* v. *Frampton* [1948] 1 K.B. 73 at 79.

[65] *Supra.* See also *Fernandes* v. *Parvardin* (1982) 264 E.G. 49 (landlord wanted property for her son. Tenants, Iranian students with a child, established greater hardship by showing that they had tried unsuccessfully to get alternative accommodation and were not eligible for council housing. The best they could hope for would be local authority temporary accommodation); *Manaton* v. *Edwards* (1985) 276 E.G. 1256 (landlord obtained possession where he was living in a caravan, and his wife had recently arrived from Russia to join him. The tenant, whose family included a baby, would be rehoused by the local authority under the Housing (Homeless Persons) Act 1977).

[66] *Baker* v. *Lewis* [1947] K.B. 186; *McIntyre* v. *Hardcastle* [1948] 2 K.B. 82.

[67] [1980] A.C. 1, *post*, p. 84.

[68] This limb of Case 9 was added after *Baker* v. *Lewis, supra*, where the foregoing propositions were accepted.

Case 10

"Where the court is satisfied that the rent charged by the tenant—

(a) for any sublet part of the dwelling-house which is a dwelling-house let on a protected tenancy or subject to a statutory tenancy is or was in excess of the maximum rent for the time being recoverable for that part, having regard to Part III of this Act, or

(b) for any sublet part of the dwelling-house which is subject to a restricted contract is or was in excess of the maximum (if any) which it is lawful for the lessor, within the meaning of Part V of this Act to require or receive having regard to the provisions of that Part."

As will be seen in Chapter 10, the rent control provisions of the 1977 Act make it unlawful for the landlord to receive rent in excess of the statutory limits. Case 10 gives the head landlord a ground for possession where the tenant who has sublet part infringes these rules. It clearly has no application where the sub-tenancy is not within the Rent Act.

The Mandatory Grounds for Possession

These are the grounds where, by section 98(2), the court *shall* make a possession order. There is no discretion to refuse if the ground is established. The mandatory grounds are set out in Part II of Schedule 15 of the 1977 Act as amended by the Housing Act 1980, and will now be considered in turn.

Case 11[69]

"Where a person (in this Case referred to as "the owner-occupier") who let the dwelling-house on a regulated tenancy had, at any time before the letting, occupied it as his residence and—

(a) not later than the relevant date[70] the landlord gave notice in writing to the tenant that possession might be recovered under this Case, and

---

[69] As amended by the Rent (Amendment) Act 1985, which by s.1(4) applies retrospectively; *Hewitt* v. *Lewis*, [1986] 1 All E.R. 927 (applies to pending applications).
[70] Defined by R.A. 1977, Sched. 15, Part III, para. 2, as being the date of the commencement of the regulated tenancy, subject to various exceptions.

    (b) the dwelling-house has not [since certain dates speci-
        fied in paragraphs (i) to (iii)] been let by the owner-
        occupier on a protected tenancy with respect to which
        the condition mentioned in paragraph (a) above was
        not satisfied, and
    (c) the court is of the opinion that of the conditions set out
        in Part V of this Schedule one of those in paragraphs
        (a) and (c) to (f) is satisfied."

The conditions referred to above are: (a) that the dwelling-house is required as a residence for the owner or any member of his family who resided with him when the last occupied it as a residence; or (c) that the owner has died and the dwelling-house is required as a residence for a member of his family who was residing with him at the time of his death; or (d) that the owner has died and the dwelling-house is required by a successor in title as his residence or for the purpose of sale with vacant possession; or (e) that a mortgagee requires the dwelling-house for the purpose of exercising the power of sale, where the mortgage was granted before the tenancy; or (f) the owner requires the dwelling-house for the purpose of sale, so that the proceeds may be used to acquire a dwelling-house more suited to his needs with regard to his place of work.[71]

It is further provided that if the main conditions (a) or (b) above are not complied with, the court may dispense with either or both of them, if of the opinion that it is just and equitable to order possession. The scope of this dispensing power will be considered below.

The purpose of Case 11 is to enable an owner-occupier who is going away for some period, for example to work abroad, to let the property during his absence, secure in the knowledge that he can recover possession on his return. In some ways Case 11 overlaps with Case 9, but the requirements are different in many respects.

Some consternation was caused by the decision of the Court of Appeal in *Pocock* v. *Steel*[72] in which it was held that Case 11 did not apply unless the landlord had resided in the property immediately prior to the current letting. The difficulty in this can be seen in the example of a landlord working abroad: if the tenant left while the landlord was still away, he would have to resume occupa-

---

[71] Conditions (c) to (f) were added by the Housing Act 1980, which is retrospective on this point, save that conditions (c) and (d) do not apply if the owner-occupier died before November 28, 1980.
[72] [1985] 1 W.L.R. 229.

tion before re-letting. This decision was quickly reversed by the Rent (Amendment) Act 1985, making it clear that the landlord's occupation need not have immediately preceded the current letting. Case 11 applies to each of a series of lettings, provided that condition (b) (which may in any event be dispensed with by the court) is satisfied, without any necessity for residence by the landlord before each of them.

It was held in *Naish* v. *Curzon*[73] that a landlord can satisfy Case 11 even though his prior residence was temporary or intermittent. Here the landlord lived mainly in South Africa for a period of years prior to the letting, but resided from time to time in the property, when visiting the country on business and for holidays. His future proposed use of the property would be similar. There was no direct authority but the "two homes"[74] cases provided some analogy. No doubt occupation of a very temporary nature, however, would not qualify as "residence" at all.

Another question which has arisen is whether the landlord must be reasonable in requiring the property as a residence. In contrast with Case 9, the word does not appear in the conditions of Case 11. It was held in *Kennealy* v. *Dunne*[75] that there is no requirement of reasonableness. It is sufficient that the landlord can show a genuine intention to occupy within a reasonable time. The fact that he does not need to do so is irrelevant.

It has already been noted that the Rent Act fails to deal expressly with the question of joint landlords or tenants. This has arisen in the context of Case 9, discussed above, and also in relation to the statutory tenancy[76] and to the resident landlord rules.[77] The issue arose in the present context in *Tilling* v. *Whiteman*,[78] where only one of joint landlords wished to resume occupation. A majority of the House of Lords, reversing the Court of Appeal, held that Case 11 was satisfied. Although the general policy of the Act was to protect the tenant, the policy of Case 11 was to encourage letting, and it should, therefore, be construed in the landlord's favour. The authorities to the contrary on Case 9, discussed above, were distinguished on the basis that the wording of that Case was different. This is a satisfactory result, as hardship would otherwise arise where, for example, a married couple let the property and subsequently separated, so that only one wished to resume occu-

[73] (1985) 273 E.G. 1221.
[74] *Ante*, p. 62.
[75] [1977] 1 Q.B. 837; (1977) 41 Conv. (N.S.) 287 (D. MacIntyre).
[76] *Ante*, p. 65.
[77] *Ante*, p. 38.
[78] [1980] A.C. 1; (1980) 39 C.L.J. 37 (K. J. Gray).

pation. It would be unfortunate if he was thereby precluded from relying on Case 11, a result which would fortuitously improve the tenant's position.

As stated above, conditions (a) and (b) may be dispensed with by the court if just and equitable to do so. In *Minay* v. *Sentongo*[79] the dispensing power was exercised where the landlord had sent a condition (a) notice, but it did not arrive. The condition was not complied with, because a notice had to be received in order to be "given" under Case 11. Similarly in *Fernandes* v. *Parvardin*,[80] where the landlord had given the tenant an oral notice, which accordingly did not satisfy condition (a). It was just and equitable to order possession, as the tenant had appreciated the position throughout. While all members of the Court of Appeal agreed that the dispensing power should be exercised, there was disagreement as to its scope. Stephenson L.J. thought the court should consider all the circumstances, including the balance of hardship. The majority view, however, was narrower, requiring the court to consider only whether any injustice or inequity flowed from the failure to comply precisely with Case 11. Where there was no misunderstanding by the tenant, there would be no such injustice or inequity, and general questions of hardship were not relevant. The matter was reviewed in *Bradshaw* v. *Baldwin-Wiseman*,[81] where property was let on an ordinary regulated tenancy which was never intended to be temporary. No condition (a) notice had been served, nor was there any suggestion at the grant that the landlord might wish to recover possession for his own use. It was held that the dispensing power was not to be exercised in such a case. The tenant must appreciate the position when he takes the property.[82] The Court of Appeal considered the views expressed in *Fernandes* v. *Parvardin*,[83] and preferred that of the minority, to the effect that all the circumstances should be examined. Here the landlord would clearly have failed on either view. So in the case of an oral condition (a) notice, the *Bradshaw* view effectively gives the court a general discretion, whereas according to the majority in *Fernandes*, the landlord is likely to succeed because no injustice flows from the failure to give written notice. If no notice at all has been given, the landlord is likely to fail on either view.[84]

---

[79] (1983) 45 P. & C.R. 190.
[80] (1982) 264 E.G. 49.
[81] (1985) 274 E.G. 285; [1985] Conv. 354 (J.E.M.).
[82] *Cf. Minay* v. *Sentongo, supra.*
[83] *Supra.*
[84] Save in the rare case where the notice has been sent but not received; *Minay* v. *Sentongo, supra.*

Finally, when possession is sought under Case 11 (or under the other mandatory grounds discussed below), an expedited procedure is available.[85] Proceedings may be commenced by originating summons, with a supporting affidavit. The period of notice between service of the application and the hearing is shorter than usual, and may be as little as seven days. The matter can be heard by a registrar and is often in chambers. However, the expedited procedure is not available where the landlord wishes to invoke the court's dispensing power, discussed above.[86]

Case 12

"Where the landlord (in this Case referred to as "the owner" intends to occupy the dwelling-house as his residence at such time as he might retire from regular employment and has let it on a regulated tenancy before he has so retired and—

(a) not later than the relevant date[87] the landlord gave notice in writing to the tenant that possession might be recovered under this Case; and

(b) the dwelling-house has not, since 14th August 1974,[88] been let by the owner on a protected tenancy to which the condition mentioned in paragraph (a) above was not satisfied; and

(c) the court is of the opinion that of the conditions set out in Part V of this Schedule one of those in paragraphs (b) to (e) is satisfied."

Paragraph (b), referred in main condition (c), is to the effect that the owner has retired from regular employment and requires the dwelling-house as a residence. Paragraphs (c) to (e)[89] are as set out in respect of Case 11, above.

As with Case 11, the court may dispense with either or both of main conditions (a) or (b) if just and equitable to order possession. The authorities on Case 11, discussed above, will presumably apply here also.

There is, as yet, no authority on Case 12. Presumably one of joint landlords may invoke it, by analogy with *Tilling* v. *White-*

---

[85] Rent Act (County Court Proceedings for Possession) Rules 1981 (S.I. 1981 No. 139).

[86] See *Minay* v. *Sentongo, supra.*

[87] See n. 70, *supra.*

[88] Case 12 was introduced by the Rent Act 1974.

[89] Paragraphs (d) and (e) were added by the Housing Act 1980.

man.[90] Difficulties could arise as to the meaning of "regular employment." For example, does it cover the self-employed?[91] Unlike Case 11, there is no requirement that the landlord should have previously resided at the property. Like Case 11, it is not necessary that the landlord's requirement of the property as a residence should be reasonable.

Case 13

"Where the dwelling-house is let under a tenancy for a term of years certain not exceeding 8 months and—

(a) not later than the relevant date[92] the landlord gave notice in writing to the tenant that possession might be recovered under this Case; and

(b) the dwelling-house was, at some time within the period of 12 months ending on the relevant date, occupied under a right to occupy it for a holiday."

This ground, therefore, permits recovery in the case of out-of-season lettings of holiday accommodation, and is designed to encourage such lettings, so that accommodation with a seasonal use may be more fully utilised. We have seen that the holiday lettings themselves are not within the Rent Act.[93] It is not necessary, however, that the holiday occupation should take the form of a letting.[94] Establishing whether the "holiday occupation" was indeed of that character could give rise to problems similar to those arising under section 9 in the case of holiday lettings.[95]

Case 14

"Where the dwelling-house is let under a tenancy for a term of years certain not exceeding 12 months and—

---

[90] [1980] A.C. 1, *supra.* Otherwise there would be hardship in the case of a married couple, if the wife did not work or retired earlier than the husband.

[91] For further problems, see Farrand and Arden, *Rent Acts and Regulations* (2nd ed.), p. 208.

[92] See n. 70, *supra.*

[93] *Ante*, p. 28.

[94] It has been suggested that the landlord's own holiday occupation would suffice; Farrand and Arden, *op. cit.*, p. 209; Yates and Hawkins, *Landlord and Tenant Law*, p. 345; *cf.* Pettit, *Private Sector Tenancies* (2nd ed.), p. 219, considering that such occupation would be based on the landlord's rights as owner, and not a "right to occupy it as a holiday." The latter view, it is submitted, is preferable.

[95] *Ante*, p. 28.

(a) not later than the relevant date[96] the landlord gave notice in writing to the tenant that possession might be recovered under this Case; and

(b) at some time within the period of 12 months ending on the relevant date, the dwelling-house was subject to such a tenancy as is referred to in section 8(1) of this Act."

Section 8 excludes institutional student lettings from protection.[97] The purpose of Case 14, therefore, is to facilitate vacation lettings of student accommodation. It is based on the same policy as Case 13.

It is not necessary that the vacation letting should be by an institutional landlord. The Case could be relied on by a private landlord who lets the property during the vacation, where during term he lets to an institution for subletting to students within section 8.

Case 15

"Where the dwelling-house is held for the purpose of being available for occupation by a minister of religion as a residence from which to perform the duties of his office and—

(a) not later than the relevant date[98] the tenant was given notice in writing that possession might be recovered under this Case, and

(b) the court is satisfied that the dwelling-house is required for occupation by a minister of religion as such a residence."

We have seen that lettings of Church of England parsonages are excluded from the Rent Act.[99] There is no such exclusion for other religions, but Case 15 provides a ground for possession in the circumstances set out above.

Cases 16 to 18

These Cases deal with the recovery of possession of dwelling-houses formerly (but not currently) occupied by persons in agricul-

---

[96] See n. 70, *supra*.
[97] *Ante*, p. 26.
[98] See n. 70, *supra*.
[99] *Ante*, p. 33.

ture, which are now required for an agricultural employee. They are outside the scope of this book.

Case 19

This concerns recovery of possession from shorthold tenants, and was dealt with in Chapter 4.

Case 20

"Where the dwelling-house was let by a person (in this Case referred to as "the owner") at any time after the commencement of section 67 of the Housing Act 1980 and—

(a) at the time when the owner acquired the dwelling-house he was a member of the regular armed forces[1] of the Crown;

(b) at the relevant date[2] the owner was a member of the regular armed forces of the Crown;

(c) not later than the relevant date the owner gave notice in writing to the tenant that possession might be recovered under this Case;

(d) the dwelling-house has not, since the commencement of section 67 of the Act of 1980 been let by the owner on a protected tenancy with respect to which the condition mentioned in paragraph (c) above was not satisfied; and

(e) the court is of the opinion that—

(i) the dwelling-house is required as a residence for the owner; or

(ii) of the conditions set out in Part V of this Schedule one of those in paragraphs (c) to (f) is satisfied."

The conditions in paragraphs (c) to (f) referred to above have been set out in the context of Case 11.

As with Cases 11 and 12, the court may dispense with either or both of main conditions (c) or (d) if it is just and equitable to make a possession order.

Unlike Case 11, the landlord need not have resided in the property prior to the letting.

---

[1] Within the meaning of section 1 of the House of Commons Disqualification Act 1975.

[2] See n. 70, *supra*.

Possession Orders

As far as the discretionary grounds under Part I of Schedule 15 are concerned, the court[3] has jurisdiction, under section 100 of the 1977 Act, either to adjourn the possession proceedings for such time as it thinks fit, or, on the making of a possession order or at any time before its execution, stay or suspend execution of the order or postpone the date of possession for such time as it thinks fit.

Unless it would cause exceptional hardship to the tenant or would be otherwise unreasonable,[4] the court must impose conditions as to payment of any arrears, rent or mesne profits and such other conditions as it thinks fit on any such adjournment, stay, suspension or postponement. If the conditions are complied with, the court may, if it thinks fit, discharge or rescind the possession order. If the tenant fails to comply with conditions imposed, for example in an adjournment, the landlord may apply for a possession order.[5] These powers of the court are commonly exercised, especially where possession is sought on the basis of rent arrears.

As mentioned above, a conditional order may be discharged if the conditions are complied with. Under a conditional order, the tenancy continues.[6] An absolute order, on the other hand (although capable of suspension or postponement) terminates the tenancy immediately.[7] An absolute order cannot be discharged, but may be converted to a conditional order and then discharged.[8]

The wide powers exercisable under section 100 do not apply to the mandatory grounds for possession. By section 89 of the Housing Act 1980, the possession order in such cases shall not be postponed (whether by the order or any variation, suspension or stay

---

[3] For the jurisdiction of the county court, see R.A. 1977, s.141. In the case of the discretionary grounds, the county court has jurisdiction even if the case is not within the normal financial limits. There is no jurisdiction to make a consent order for possession unless the tenant concedes that the Rent Act does not apply; *R.* v. *Bloomsbury & Marylebone County Court, ex p. Blackburne* (1985) 275 E.G. 1273. See also *Syed Hussain Bin Abdul Rahman Bin Shaikh Alkaff* v. *A. M. Abdullah Sahib & Co.* [1985] 1 W.L.R. 1392 (P.C.).

[4] For examples, see Farrand & Arden, *Rent Acts and Regulations* (2nd ed.), pp. 130–131.

[5] *Mills* v. *Allen* [1953] 2 Q.B. 341.

[6] *Sherrin* v. *Brand* [1956] 1 Q.B. 403 (successor could acquire tenancy on death of tenant where order conditional).

[7] *American Economic Laundry* v. *Little* [1951] 1 K.B. 400 (where tenant died before execution of order, no successor could acquire the tenancy).

[8] *Payne* v. *Cooper* [1958] 1 Q.B. 174; *Mills* v. *Allen, supra.*

of execution) to a date later than 14 days after the making of the order, unless exceptional hardship would be caused by requiring possession to be given up by that date. In such circumstances it shall not be postponed beyond six weeks from the making of the order.

The final point to consider is the position of the tenant's spouse. It is provided by section 75 of the Housing Act 1980[9] that if a tenancy is terminated by possession proceedings at a time when the tenant's spouse or former spouse, having rights of occupation under the Matrimonial Homes Act (now the Act of 1983),[10] is occupying the dwelling-house, then the spouse or former spouse shall have the same rights in relation to any adjournment, stay, suspension or postponement, so long as he or she remains in occupation, as he or she would have if those rights of occupation were not affected by the termination of the tenancy. The spouse, therefore, has *locus standi* to apply to court for the exercise of its powers of suspension, postponement and so forth.

Termination Apart from the Grounds for Possession

In addition to the grounds for possession, there are certain other circumstances in which protected and statutory tenants may cease to enjoy Rent Act security of tenure. As we have seen, a statutory tenancy terminates if the tenant ceases to reside, although his liabilities continue until he gives proper notice under section 3 to the landlord.[11] We have also seen that bankruptcy does not terminate a statutory tenancy, but does prevent a statutory tenancy arising where a protected tenant's trustee in bankruptcy terminates the protected tenancy by disclaimer.[12] Other circumstances requiring discussion include the following:

(i) Unfit houses

The Housing Act 1985 [13] provides that nothing in the Rent Act shall prevent recovery of possession while a closing order is in

---

[9] Reversing *Penn* v. *Dunn* [1970] 2 Q.B. 686. See also *Grange Lane South Flats Ltd.* v. *Cook* (1979) 254 E.G. 499.

[10] These rights terminate on divorce. As to transfer on divorce, see *ante*, p. 67.

[11] *Ante*, p. 67. See also *Hulme* v. *Langford* (1985) 50 P. & C.R. 199, *ante*, p. 61.

[12] *Ante*, p. 55.

[13] s.276. The position is similar in relation to overcrowding (R.A. 1977, s.101, *ante*, p. 69). See also H.A. 1985, s.264 (undertakings); s.270 (demolition orders); s.286 (obstructive buildings orders); s.368 (inadequate fire escapes); s.612 (housing powers).

force. The policy of public health statutes overrides that of the Rent Act. The tenant cannot resist the possession action even if the disrepair which has given rise to the closing order is the landlord's fault.[14]

(ii) Change of user

A tenancy which is initially a protected tenancy under the Rent Act will cease to be so protected if a change of user brings it within some other code of statutory protection, for example those relating to business tenancies or agricultural holdings, thereby excluding it from the Rent Act. So in *Cheryl Investments Ltd.* v. *Saldanha*[15] a protected tenant who equipped the dwelling-house for business lost Rent Act protection, as the tenancy now qualified as a business tenancy under the Landlord and Tenant Act 1954, Part II. The landlord in such cases may recover possession (if at all) under that Act.

(iii) Change in status of occupier

A protected or statutory tenancy will cease if the tenancy ceases to be a tenant, for example by becoming a licensee, whereupon the tenancy is surrendered by operation of law.[16] Any arrangement whereby it is alleged that a tenant has become a licensee will be closely scrutinised, but there is no presumption of undue influence between landlord and tenant.[17]

Similarly if the tenant acquires title against the landlord under the Limitation Act 1980 by failing to pay rent for the necessary period.[18] It has been held, however, that a statutory sub-tenancy does not terminate as against the head landlord where possessory title is acquired as against the tenant.[19]

(iv) Eviction by a person not bound by the tenancy

This involves the situation where the landlord is a mortgagor, whose mortgage prohibits the power of leasing. Any tenancy granted binds the landlord (by estoppel) but does not bind the

---

[14] *Buswell* v. *Goodwin* [1971] 1 W.L.R. 92.
[15] [1978] 1 W.L.R. 1329, *ante*, p. 32.
[16] *Foster* v. *Robinson* [1951] 1 K.B. 149. A mere agreement to become a licensee would not suffice.
[17] *Mathew* v. *Bobbins* (1980) 41 P. & C.R. 1.
[18] The Act extends to statutory tenants; *Jessamine Investment Co.* v. *Schwartz* [1978] Q.B. 264.
[19] *Jessamine Investment Co.* v. *Schwartz, supra.*

mortgagee, who can recover possession.[20] The position is, of course, otherwise if the tenancy was granted before the mortgage,[21] or if the mortgagee has accepted the tenant, or, it has been held, if the mortgagee seeks possession otherwise than in good faith.[22] It has been suggested that the mortgagee cannot recover possession where the tenancy has become statutory, but this, it is submitted, is doubtful.[23]

This may be contrasted with the position where the immediate reversion is transferred to a body not bound by the Rent Act, for example, the Crown.[24] Here the tenancy will bind the new landlord (to the extent that it can do so under the general law), but the Rent Act will cease to apply.

(v) Destruction of the premises

In the case of a protected tenancy, destruction of the premises will not terminate the tenancy, unless the doctrine of frustration applies.[25] Where the tenancy is statutory, however, it will come to an end on destruction of the premises, as the tenant can no longer occupy the dwelling-house as his residence.[26] If, on the other hand, the premises are merely uninhabitable, the statutory tenancy continues, provided the tenant intends to return.[27]

(vi) Other cases

Another possibility may be where the premises are subject to an enforcement notice following a breach of planning control under the Town and Country Planning Act 1971.

Other cases involve the situation where the tenancy does not terminate, but ceases to be subject to the Rent Act. This would occur if the rent falls below two-thirds of the rateable value on the "appropriate day."[28] Similarly if the Secretary of State should

---

[20] *Dudley and District Benefit Building Society* v. *Emerson* [1949] Ch. 707.
[21] Even where the "landlord" had no title at the grant of the tenancy; *Church of England Building Society* v. *Piskor* [1954] Ch. 553.
[22] *Quennell* v. *Maltby* [1979] 1 W.L.R. 318.
[23] (1977) 41 Conv. (N.S.) 197 (P. Smith), relying on *Jessamine Investment Co.* v. *Schwartz*, *supra*; *cf.* correspondence at [1978] Conv. 322.
[24] *Ante*, p. 30.
[25] This will rarely be the case; *National Carriers Ltd.* v. *Panalpina (Northern) Ltd.* [1981] A.C. 675.
[26] *Ellis & Sons Amalgamated Properties Ltd.* v. *Sisman* [1948] 1 K.B. 653.
[27] *Morleys (Birmingham) Ltd.* v. *Slater* [1950] 1 K.B. 506 (war damage).
[28] *Ante*, pp. 22–23 and n.64.

exercise his powers under section 143[29] of the 1977 Act, whereupon dwelling-houses in areas specified in his order would cease to
be the subject of a regulated tenancy.

[29] *Ante*, p. 34. Any former protected tenancy would continue to exist
under the general law. Any statutory tenancy would apparently terminate, but subject to transitional provisions under s.143(2), which
expressly refers to provisions to avoid or mitigate hardship.

Chapter 7

STATUTORY TENANTS BY SUCCESSION

Although, as we have seen, the statutory tenancy is a personal right which is not assignable,[1] it is nevertheless capable of transmission on death. This can occur on the death of the original tenant, and again on the death of the first successor. Hence the landlord might be unable to recover possession for a very considerable period. The purpose of the succession rules is to further the policy of the Rent Act that the tenant should enjoy security of tenure in his home. His security would be seriously impaired if the landlord could eject his family, for example his elderly widow, on his death. It is questionable, however, whether a second succession is justifiable. It might be noted that the more recent legislation conferring security on public sector tenants permits only one succession to the tenancy.[2] In another context, succession rights to tenancies of agricultural holdings have been withdrawn by the Agricultural Holdings Act 1984 save in respect of tenancies granted before that Act.

The current provisions are contained in Schedule 1 of the 1977 Act, as amended by the Housing Act 1980. They apply on the death of a person ("the original tenant") who, immediately before his death, was a protected tenant of the dwelling-house or the statutory tenant of it by virtue of his previous tenancy.

The First Successor

In respect of deaths after November 28, 1980,[3] the first successor is the surviving spouse (if any) of the original tenant, if residing[4] in the dwelling-house immediately before the death of the original tenant. The spouse is the statutory tenant "if and so long as he or she occupies the dwelling-house as his or her residence."[5] If there is no such spouse, the first successor is a person who was "a member of the original tenant's family," residing with him at his death

---

[1] *Ante*, Chap. 5.
[2] H.A. 1985, s.87.
[3] When the amendments contained in H.A. 1980, s.76 came into effect.
[4] Temporary absence, such as where the spouse is in hospital at the death, may be disregarded; *Tompkins* v. *Rowley* (1949) 153 E.G. 442.
[5] This requirement is identical to that of s.2, and thus imports the test laid down in *Brown* v. *Brash* [1948] 2 K.B. 247, *ante*, p. 58.

and for the period of six months immediately before his death. Such a person is the statutory tenant if and so long as he occupies the dwelling-house as his residence. If there is more than one claimant, then the successor may be decided by agreement,[6] or, in default of agreement, by the county court. Again, the position may be contrasted with the public sector, where family members other than the spouse must have resided with the tenant for twelve months prior to the death and, if there is more than one claimant, the successor is selected by the landlord in default of agreement between the claimants.

The position prior to the amendments effected by the Housing Act 1980 was that the tenant's widow took priority. A widower could only claim as a "member of the family," in competition with any other such member. Another difference was that the widow must have resided *with* the tenant at his death. The effect of the 1980 amendment, therefore, is to include separated spouses who live under the same roof but not together.

The Second Successor

If the first successor continued to be the statutory tenant until his death, then similar rules apply on his death. That is, any surviving spouse takes priority if residing in the dwelling-house at the death of the first successor. In the absence of any such spouse, the second successor is a member of the first successor's family who resided with him for six months immediately prior to his death. In the event of more than one such member, the position is as mentioned above in the case of the first succession. The Housing Act 1980 made the same amendments in respect of the spouse as have been discussed in respect of the first succession.

Where, after the succession, a new contractual tenancy is granted to the successor, this cannot operate to increase the number of successions. In the case of a new grant to a first successor, there can be one further succession on his death. In the case of a new grant to a second successor, there can be no further succession on his death.[7]

Where no succession rights arise on the death of a statutory tenant (because he was the second successor or because no person qualifies as a successor), then any person who continues to occupy the dwelling-house is protected by section 3 of the Protection from

---

[6] The agreement is that of the claimants. The landlord has no right to participate.
[7] R.A. 1977, Sched. 1, para. 10.

Eviction Act 1977, whereby it is unlawful for the landlord to enforce his right to recover possession without a court order. Where a statutory tenant dies in circumstances where there can be no transmission of the tenancy, presumably his personal representatives should give notice to the landlord under section 3(3) of the Rent Act 1977.[8]

Devolution of Contractual Tenancy

As noted above, the succession rules come into operation whether the original tenancy was statutory or still protected at the tenant's death. If it was a protected tenancy, then it will pass to some beneficiary under the tenant's will or upon his intestacy. This beneficiary may or may not be the same person as the first successor. The somewhat curious result, it has been held, is that the protected, *i.e.* contractual, tenancy "goes into abeyance" for the period during which a statutory tenancy by succession is in operation. In *Moodie* v. *Hosegood*[9] a protected tenant died intestate, whereupon the tenancy vested in the Probate judge under section 9 of the Administration of Estates Act 1925. His widow continued to reside in the house. The landlord, having determined the contractual tenancy by serving notice to quit on the Probate judge, sought to recover possession from the widow. The House of Lords upheld her claim to remain in possession as statutory tenant by succession. Lord Morton explained the position as follows: "if a contractual tenancy is still subsisting at her husband's death, and devolves on someone other than the widow, it is not destroyed but the rights and obligations which would ordinarily devolve upon the successor in title of the contractual tenant are suspended, so long as the widow retains possession of the dwelling-house."[10] Thus a notice to quit given to or by the contractual tenant in such circumstances will not affect the successor's rights. If the statutory tenant by succession remains in residence beyond the termination of the contractual tenancy, then the person entitled to the contractual tenancy under the general law will never enjoy any rights. If, however, the contractual tenancy continues until the end of any statutory tenancy by succession, then the rights and obligations under it will "revive."

---

[8] By analogy with *Boyer* v. *Warbey* [1953] 1 Q.B. 234 and *King's College, Cambridge* v. *Kershman* (1948) 64 T.L.R. 547, *ante*, p. 67.
[9] [1952] A.C. 61.
[10] *Ibid.* at p. 74. See further Megarry's *Rent Acts* (10th ed.), pp. 221–225.

A further problem arises where the person entitled under the general law to succeed to the contractual tenancy is the same person as the statutory tenant by succession. In what capacity does he continue to occupy? If he takes as statutory tenant by succession, there can only be one further transmission. If he can be regarded as occupying in right of the protected tenancy, then there may be two further transmissions after his death. This was the position in *Whitmore* v. *Lambert*,[11] where the protected tenant's widow was entitled under his will, and under the statutory succession provisions. She continued to reside, but did not prove the will. It was held that she had taken as contractual tenant, so that on her death a statutory tenant by succession could take as if on the death of an original tenant.

The Meaning of "Family"

Most of the litigation on the successor provisions is concerned with the meaning of "family," which is not defined by the 1977 Act.[12] In the public sector, on the other hand, where a member of the tenant's "family" can similarly succeed to the secure tenancy, there is a statutory definition[13] which, if contained in the Rent Act, would have resolved most (but perhaps not all) of the problems discussed below. In the private sector, the meaning of "family" must be gleaned from the case-law, much of which concerns the rights of persons cohabiting with the tenant outside marriage. In *Gammans* v. *Ekins*[14] the tenant's "common law husband" failed in his claim to succeed to the tenancy. Moralistic overtones can be detected in the judgments of the Court of Appeal, Asquith L.J. thought it "anomalous that a person can

---

[11] [1955] 1 W.L.R. 495.
[12] Nor, for that matter, is "spouse" defined. In the absence of any extending definition, "spouse" presumably means a party to a valid (including voidable, but not void) marriage, which subsisted until the tenant's death. As will be seen, it does not include a "common law" spouse. Nor, presumably, does it include a polygamous spouse (although such a person could claim as a "member of the family").
[13] H.A. 1985, s.113, providing that a person is a member of another's family if he is the spouse, parent, grandparent, child, grandchild, brother, sister, uncle, aunt, nephew or niece, or if they live together as husband and wife. Any relationship by marriage is treated as a relationship by blood, and any relationship of the half-blood is treated as a relationship of the whole blood. "Child" includes stepchild, and an illegitimate person is treated as the legitimate child of his mother and reputed father.
[14] [1950] 2 K.B. 328.

acquire a 'status of irremovability' by living or having lived in sin . . . . To say of two people masquerading,[15] as these two were, as husband and wife . . . that they were members of the same family, seems to be an abuse of the English language."[16] The couple had no children. It was left open whether this would have made any difference. This point arose in *Hawes* v. *Evendon*,[17] where a woman who had cohabited with the tenant for 12 years and had two children by him was held to be a member of his family. The Court of Appeal reviewed the authorities in *Dyson Holdings Ltd.* v. *Fox*,[18] where the claimant had lived with the tenant as his wife for some 40 years, but had no children. In 1940 they moved into the property in question. At his death in 1961 the tenant was a statutory tenant of the property. The claimant stayed on after his death until 1973, when the landlords, having discovered that the couple were never married, sought possession. It was held that the claimant was entitled to remain in occupation as statutory tenant by succession. The word "family" should not be construed in a technical or legal sense, but in the sense that would be attributed to it by the ordinary man in the street at the time relevant to the decision of the particular case.[19] In view of the stability and permanence of their relationship, the claimant would popularly have been considered to be a member of the tenant's family at his death. Not every "mistress," it was added, should be so regarded. Relationships of a casual or intermittent nature and those bearing indications of impermanence would not come within the popular concept of a family unit. Lord Denning M.R. found the distinction between couples with children and those without "ridiculous."[20] The court was at liberty to reject the distinction, in spite of *Gammans* v. *Ekins*,[21] because, owing to the lapse of time since that case was decided, and the change in social conditions, the decision was not in accord with modern thinking. As James L.J. put it, "The popular meaning given to the word 'family' is not fixed once

---

[15] This expression was considered unhelpful in *Watson* v. *Lucas* [1980] 1 W.L.R. 1493, *infra*.

[16] [1950] 2 K.B. 328, at 331. See also Evershed M.R. at 334.

[17] [1953] 1 W.L.R. 1169.

[18] [1976] Q.B. 503.

[19] As Lord Denning M.R. said, at p. 508, "It is not used in the sense in which it would be used by a studious and unwordly lawyer, but in the sense in which it would be used by a man who is 'base, common and popular,' to use Shakespeare's words in Henry V, Act IV, Scene 1. . . ."

[20] *Ibid.* at p. 509.

[21] *Supra*.

and for all time. I have no doubt that with the passage of years it has changed. The cases reveal that it is not restricted to blood relationships and those created by the marriage ceremony. It can include *de facto* as well as *de jure* relationships."[22] Bridge L.J. felt some hesitation as to whether the court could give effect to the change in social attitude without doing violence to the doctrine of judicial precedent, but in the end concluded that it would be unduly legalistic to allow this consideration to defeat the claim.

The view that a change in social attitude can change the meaning of a statutory provision has not been accepted without reservation in subsequent decisions. The difficulty is highlighted by Oliver L.J. in his dissenting judgment in *Watson* v. *Lucas*,[23] where he explained that the relevant time for determining the matter in *Dyson Holdings Ltd.* v. *Fox*[24] was upon the tenant's death in 1961. At that time *Gammans* v. *Ekins*[25] could not be regarded as no longer binding, because it had been subsequently applied in 1964 by a unanimous Court of Appeal in *Ross* v. *Collins*,[26] which was cited in *Dyson* but not referred to in the judgments.

The question of cohabiting couples next came before the Court of Appeal in *Helby* v. *Rafferty*,[27] where the male claimant had lived with the female tenant for the five years preceding her death. His claim failed, as, on the particular facts, the relationship lacked the element of permanence. The tenant had valued her independance and had deliberately chosen to avoid a permanent relationship. The parties had no intention of marrying, and did not hold themselves out as married.[28] While the absence of children was not fatal to the claim, their existence might indicate a family unit. Other relevant factors would be whether the woman adopted the man's name and whether the couple encouraged people to regard them as married. *Dyson Holdings Ltd.* v. *Fox*[29] was distinguished, and all three judges criticised that decision in so far as it held that a change of social habit could alter the meaning of a statute.

The issue arose again before the Court of Appeal in *Watson* v.

---

[22] [1976] Q.B. 503, at 511.
[23] [1980] 1 W.L.R. 1493. See, however, (1980) 96 L.Q.R. 248, at pp. 265–266 (A.A.S. Zuckerman). The matter was left open by the House of Lords in *Carega Properties S.A.* v. *Sharratt, infra.*
[24] *Supra.*
[25] *Supra.*
[26] [1964] 1 W.L.R. 425.
[27] [1979] 1 W.L.R. 13.
[28] It seems, then, that the claimant might have succeeded if the couple had "masqueraded" as husband and wife; *cf. Gammans* v. *Ekins, supra.*
[29] *Supra.*

Lucas,[30] where *Dyson* was applied, but was regarded as not to be extended. The male claimant had lived with the woman tenant until her death nearly 20 years later. They did not hold themselves out as married, and had no children. The majority upheld the claim. The relationship was permanent even though the woman had not adopted the man's name, and the man had a wife (from whom he had never been divorced) and children living elsewhere. These factors were outweighed by the lasting nature of the relationship. Use of the same name, or the presence of children, would favour the claim, but the reverse was not necessarily true. As far as the wife and children elsewhere were concerned, it was possible to be a member of more than one family, but it was said to be impossible to reside with more than one for the purpose of succession to a tenancy.[31]

There is, as yet, no authority on the question whether the surviving member of a homosexual couple could succeed to the tenancy under the Rent Act. The matter has arisen in the context of secure tenancies under the Housing Act 1985. In *Harrogate Borough Council* v. *Simpson*[32] the claim of the surviving member of a lesbian couple failed. The wording of the two statutes is different, the Housing Act including in its definition of "family" persons who "live together as husband and wife."[33] It is not surprising that the claimant was regarded as outside the definition. Had the matter arisen under the Rent Act, it is suggested that the result would have been similar. Even taking the widest sense of "family" as expressed in *Dyson Holdings Ltd.* v. *Fox*,[34] from which, as we have seen, there has been a retreat, it is unlikely that the claimant would have succeeded. Lord Fraser of Tullybelton, in dismissing the application for leave to appeal to the House of Lords in the *Simpson* case, said "It seems to me that you are fighting for a social revolution, but that is more than the courts can do. It is a matter for Parliament. I do not accept that when Parliament passed the Housing Act 1980 [now the Act of 1985] they meant a homosexual couple to be treated as husband and wife."[35]

So far we have discussed the extent to which cohabiting couples can be regarded as "family." It remains to consider how far other

---

[30] [1980] 1 W.L.R. 1493; [1980] Conv.78 (A. Sydenham).
[31] *Cf. Morgan* v. *Murch* [1970] 1 W.L.R. 778, holding that it was possible to reside in more than one place. See also Pettit, *Private Sector Tenancies* (2nd ed,), p. 95, doubting the proposition in *Watson* v. *Lucas*.
[32] *The Times*, December 14, 1984; [1985] Conv. 355 (J.E.M.).
[33] H.A. 1985, s.113.
[34] *Supra*.
[35] *The Times*, March 1, 1985.

relationships are included. Clearly such relationships as parents, children,[36] brothers and sisters[37] are included, but the mere fact of a blood relationship is not necessarily sufficient. In *Langdon* v. *Horton*[38] it was held that the tenant's two first cousins, who had lived with her for many years, were not members of her "family."

As far as *de facto* relationships are concerned (*i.e.* where there is no legal relationship by blood or marriage), the most recent authority is the decision of the House of Lords in *Carega Properties S.A. (formerly Joram Developments Ltd.)* v. *Sharratt*.[39] The tenant was an elderly widow. The claimant was a young man who had moved in with her and stayed for nearly 20 years, until her death. The parties had a platonic *de facto* "aunt/nephew" relationship. In rejecting the man's claim, the House of Lords held that the only *de facto* relationships which were recognised for succession purposes were the "common law" spouse and the parent/child relationship where the child was young, for example where the child had not been legally adopted.[40] Two adults having a platonic relationship could not be regarded as "family" by acting, for example, as brother and sister or father and daughter.[41] Such persons were members of the same household, but not members of the same family. Step and in-law relations, however, might qualify.[42]

The Meaning of "Residing with" the Tenant

As we have seen, the requirements are different according to whether the claimant is the tenant's spouse or a member of his family. The spouse need only show residence in the dwelling-house immediately before the death, while a member of the family must show residence *with* the tenant for the period of six months

---

[36] Including illegitimate, adopted (whether legally or *de facto*) and step-children; *Brock* v. *Wollams* [1949] 2 K.B. 388.
[37] *Price* v. *Gould* (1930) 143 L.T. 333.
[38] [1951] 1 K.B. 66.
[39] [1979] 1 W.L.R. 928; (1980) 39 C.L.J. 31 (P. Tennant); (1980) 96 L.Q.R. 248 at 260–268 (A.A.S. Zuckerman). Ironically, the tenant was the widow of Salter J. who had pondered the meaning of "family" in *Salter* v. *Lask* [1925] 1 K.B. 584.
[40] See *Brock* v. *Wollams* [1949] 2 K.B. 388; *Jones* v. *Whitehill* [1950] 2 K.B. 204. It is not clear whether a claimant who is still a child at the tenant's death can succeed to the tenancy. No legal estate is involved, but contractual obligations are owed to the landlord.
[41] See *Ross* v. *Collins* [1964] 1 W.L.R. 425.
[42] *Ross* v. *Collins, supra*, approved and applied by the House of Lords in *Carega Properties S.A.* v. *Sharratt*.

immediately prior to the death. In *Foreman* v. *Beagley*[43] the tenant had been in hospital for the last three years of her life. Her son took up residence during the last year. His claim failed. He came in as a "caretaker," and there had never been any community of living with his mother. It might have been otherwise if he had lived with her before her illness and had continued to live there during her absence.

Physical absence of the claimant, for example in hospital or on military service, may be disregarded if his intention to reside is continuing.[44]

The mere fact of residence in the same dwelling-house is not sufficient to establish residence with the tenant. Hence the claimant will not succeed if he was a sub-tenant of part of the property, sharing some rooms with the tenant.[45] However, the claimant (the tenant's granddaughter) succeeded in *Collier* v. *Stoneman*[46] where she had little contact with the tenant, having her own room but sharing the kitchen.

More than one Member of the Family

As stated above, the position where more than one claimant is qualified to succeed to the tenancy is that the county court decides who is the successor, in default of agreement between the claimants. There is no question of joint successors. In *Dealex Properties Ltd.* v. *Brooks*,[47] decided at a time when the wording of the statutory provision was less clear than under the 1977 Act, Harman L.J. said that joint successors would lead to "fearful confusion." There would be a "sort of tontine which will last for so long as the survivor of them is in existence. I think that under the Rent Acts a tenant must be a single person because it is a status of irremovability which belongs to him, and I do not think to anyone but him."[48] Diplock L.J. also feared that any other construction would lead to "absurd consequences."[49] In so far as a statutory tenancy may be

---

[43] [1969] 1 W.L.R. 1387. See also *Morgan* v. *Murch* [1970] 1 W.L.R. 778, where the tenant's son deserted his wife and returned to his mother. He was held to be residing with his mother even though he remained the tenant of his former matrimonial home.

[44] *Middleton* v. *Bull* [1951] W.N. 517; *Tompkins* v. *Rowley* (1949) 153 E.G. 442.

[45] *Edmunds* v. *Jones* [1957] 1 W.L.R. 1118n.

[46] [1957] 1 W.L.R. 1108.

[47] [1966] 1 Q.B. 542.

[48] *Ibid.* at p. 551.

[49] *Ibid.* at p. 554.

held jointly,[50] this reasoning is not convincing, but the statute is clear. In the public sector, there is equally no provision for joint successors, although the position is different in that, in default of agreement, the landlord selects the successor.[51]

The agreement between the claimants as to who is the successor may be inferred.[52] Pending any such agreement, the statutory tenancy exists although the identity of the tenant is not settled. In *Williams* v. *Williams*[53] the parties failed to agree, whereupon the matter fell to be decided by the county court. The claimants were the tenant's son and her widower (the case being decided at a time when a widower had no priority over other family members). The son had treated the tenant well, while the widower had treated her badly. But the son was not in financial need, whereas the widower was. On appeal, the widower's claim was upheld. His needs outweighed the son's merits, although hardship was not the sole test.

Where the Original Tenants were Joint Tenants

The final matter to be considered is a somewhat problematical area which has yet to be fully considered by the courts. It may be that only one of the joint protected tenants becomes the statutory tenant,[54] in which case the successor rules will presumably apply in the ordinary way. More difficult is the situation where both tenants become statutory tenants. If both die together, there seems no reason why the successor rules should not apply, but must the successor be a member of the family of both tenants? Probably this is not required, as a literal construction of the Act has not found favour in other contexts involving joint tenants (or landlords).[55]

More likely is the situation where one joint statutory tenant dies. Again, the question arises whether any person claiming as successor must be a member of the family of both tenants. More fundamentally, can the rules apply at all? It might be considered that the survivor becomes sole statutory tenant, to the exclusion of the claims of any successor. If the successor rules do operate, presumably the successor takes jointly with the survivor.[56] It is indeed

---

[50] See *Lloyd* v. *Sadler* [1978] Q.B. 774, *ante,* p. 65.

[51] H.A. 1985, s.89(2).

[52] *Dealex Properties Ltd.* v. *Brooks, supra*; *Trayfoot* v. *Lock* [1957] 1 W.L.R. 351.

[53] [1970] 1 W.L.R. 1530.

[54] *Lloyd* v. *Sadler, supra.*

[55] *Lloyd* v. *Sadler, supra*; *Tilling* v. *Whiteman* [1980] A.C. 1; *ante,* p. 84; *Halford's Executors* v. *Boden, infra.*

[56] *Cf.* comments in *Dealex Properties Ltd.* v. *Brooks, supra.*

difficult to see how the successor rules could apply if one of the joint tenants dies while the tenancy is still protected. The contractual tenancy could not go into abeyance[57] in such circumstances. The survivor would become sole protected tenant, and it is doubtful whether the protected tenancy could coexist with a statutory tenancy by succession.[58]

Some assistance may be derived from *Halford's Executors* v. *Boden,*[59] where the child of a deserted spouse was held entitled as successor where the tenancy had been held jointly by both spouses. The "residing with" condition was satisfied if the claimant had resided with one of the joint tenants.

These matter have to some extent been provided for by statute in the case of public sector secure tenancies. By section 88 of the Housing Act 1985, there can be no succession where an original joint tenant has become the sole tenant. An amendment to the Rent Act, either adopting this provision or otherwise clarifying the position, would be welcome.

---

[57] *Ante,* p. 97.
[58] See further [1978] Conv. 436 at 440–441 (J. Martin); Megarry's *Rent Acts* (10th ed.) at 218.
[59] (1953) 103 L.J. News. 768 (county court).

Chapter 8

RESTRICTED CONTRACTS

We have seen that, prior to 1974, furnished tenancies were outside the full protection of the Rent Act.[1] Instead, furnished tenancies and certain other tenancies and licences enjoyed the more limited protection of what is now known as the restricted contract régime. Since the Rent Act 1974, most furnished tenancies have become regulated tenancies. That Act introduced the distinction between tenancies granted by resident and non-resident landlords, the latter category being fully protected, whether furnished or unfurnished. Tenancies granted by resident landlords have now replaced furnished tenancies as the principal example of restricted contracts. The definition, as we will see, embraces these and certain other tenancies and licences which are outside the regulated tenancy code.

The restricted contract provisions are the only part of the Rent Act which confers any protection on licensees. This will perhaps be less important since the decision in *Street* v. *Mountford*,[2] after which it will be more difficult to establish that the occupier is indeed a licensee and not a tenant.

As will be explained below, the protection conferred by the restricted contract code consists primarily of rent control. Restricted contracts entered into before the Housing Act 1980 enjoyed limited security of tenure, but this has been removed by the 1980 Act in respect of restricted contracts entered into subsequently. Such contracts merely have the benefit of the requirement of a court order for possession, which may be suspended for a maximum of three months.

Definition of a Restricted Contract

By section 19(2) of the Rent Act 1977, a restricted contract is a contract "whereby one person grants to another person, in consideration of a rent which includes payment for the use of furniture

---

[1] *Ante,* p. 2. Furnished tenancies were within the jurisdiction of rent tribunals between the Furnished Houses (Rent Control) Act 1946 and the Rent Act 1974.

[2] [1985] A.C. 809, *ante*, p. 10.

or for services, the right to occupy a dwelling as a residence." Section 19(6) further provides that a contract within the above description and relating to a dwelling which consists of only part of a house is a restricted contract "whether or not the lessee is entitled, in addition to exclusive occupation of that part, to the use in common with any other person of other rooms or accommodation in the house."

For the purpose of section 19, "dwelling" means a house[3] or part of a house; "lessor" and "lessee" mean the person who grants or is granted, under a restricted contract, the right to occupy the dwelling as a residence and any person directly or indirectly deriving title from him; and "services" includes attendance,[4] the provision of heating or lighting, the supply of hot water and any other privilege or facility connected with the occupancy of a dwelling, other than a privilege or facility requisite for the purposes of access, cold water supply or sanitary accommodation.[5]

It will be noticed that, although the occupation cannot be rent-free, there is no requirement that the rent must be at least two-thirds of the rateable value on the appropriate day.[6] Nor is there any requirement that a substantial part of the rent be attributable to furniture or services,[7] although the *de minimis* principle applies. Since the Rent Act 1974, bringing furnished tenancies into protection, the continuing presence of furniture in the definition of a restricted contract seems to have lost its rationale. Other implications of the definition in section 19 will be further discussed after a consideration of those tenancies and licences which are expressly excluded from the definition.

Exclusions

(i) High rateable value

The restricted contract code does not apply to a dwelling which is above the rateable value limits. The limits are similar to those applicable to regulated tenancies, but are not identical. The higher of the alternative rateable values mentioned below applies if the dwelling is in Greater London.[8]

---

[3] This includes a hotel, even if purpose–built; *Luganda* v. *Service Hotels Ltd.* [1969] 2 Ch. 209.
[4] See *ante*, p. 26.
[5] R.A. 1977, s.19(8).
[6] As is required of regulated tenancies, *ante*, p. 22.
[7] *cf.* s.7, *ante*, p. 25.
[8] R.A. 1977, s.19(3), (4).

Where the appropriate day[9] in relation to the dwelling is on or after April 1, 1973, the dwelling is excluded if its rateable value exceeded £1,500 or £750 on the appropriate day. Where the appropriate day fell before April 1, 1973, the dwelling is excluded if on the appropriate day its rateable value exceed £400 or £200 and exceeded £1,500 or £750 on April 1, 1973.

(ii) Regulated tenancy

A contract cannot be a restricted contract if it satisfies the definition of a regulated tenancy.[10] As the two codes are incompatible in relation to rent control and security of tenure, they are mutually exclusive.

(iii) Local authority and similar contracts

This exclusion was introduced by the Housing Act 1980,[11] reversing the decision in *Lambeth L.B.C.* v. *Udechuka.*[12] It is now provided that the restricted contract rules cannot apply where the lessor's interest belongs to a body mentioned in section 14 of the 1977 Act,[13] thus excluding contracts entered into by local authorities and similar bodies.

(iv) The Crown and government departments

As in the case of regulated tenancies, there is an exclusion where the interest of the lessor belongs to the Crown or to a government deparment. Since the Housing Act 1980, the exclusion no longer applies to the Duchies of Lancaster or Cornwall, nor to the Crown Estate Commissioners.[14]

(v) Substantial board

A contract cannot be a restricted contract if the rent includes payment in respect of board if the value of the board to the lessee forms a substantial proportion of the whole rent.[15] The meaning of

[9] *Ibid.* s.25(3); *ante*, p. 21.
[10] *Ibid.* s.19(5).
[11] Amending R.A. 1977, s.19(5).
[12] *The Times,* April 30, 1980 (concerning the validity of a notice to quit).
[13] *Ante*, p. 31. Thus there is no overlap with the secure tenancy code.
[14] R.A. 1977, s.19(5), as amended by H.A. 1980, s.73(2).
[15] *Ibid.*

"board" and "substantial" were discussed in Chapter 2, in the context of section 7.[16] There we saw that a tenancy cannot be a regulated tenancy if there is any board (which is more than *de minimis*). Instead, it falls within the restricted code unless the board element is substantial. We also saw that a tenancy cannot be regulated if there is substantial attendance.[17] There is no exclusion from the restricted contract code on the ground of attendance, whether or not substantial. Thus an occupier in receipt of substantial board is completely outside the protection of the Rent Act. Non-substantial board and substantial attendance bring the occupier within the restricted contract régime, while non-substantial attendance does not preclude the establishment of a regulated tenancy.

(vi) Rent (Agriculture) Act 1976

Section 19(5) also excludes from the definition of a restricted contract a protected occupancy as defined in the Rent (Agriculture) Act 1976. This Act gave security of tenure to farm-workers and their families who lived in tied accommodation in England and Wales.

(vii) Housing Association etc. tenancies

The restricted contract code cannot apply to a tenancy where the interest of the landlord belongs to a housing association or housing trust, or to the Housing Corporation.[18] This provision, resulting from a Law Commission recommendation,[19] cured an inconvenient overlap whereby furnished lettings of housing associations were subject to two conflicting systems of rent control.

(viii) Occupation for a holiday

By section 19(7), no right to occupy a dwelling for a holiday shall be treated as a right to occupy it as a residence. This is similar to the exclusion from the regulated tenancy code of holiday lettings.[20] No doubt similar difficulties may be encountered here as to the meaning of "holiday," as discussed in Chapter 2.

---

[16] *Ante*, pp. 25–26.
[17] This term was explained at p. 26, *ante*, in the context of s.7.
[18] R.A. 1977, s.19(5).
[19] Law Com. No. 81, para. 5, Cmnd. 6751 (1977).
[20] R.A. 1977, s.9, *ante*, p. 28.

(ix) Exclusion by ministerial order

As in the case of regulated tenancies,[21] the Secretary of State
has power by order to provide that section 19 shall not apply to
dwellings exceeding a specified rateable value.[22] This power is, as
yet, unexercised.

Although not specifically mentioned in the Act, it appears that
contracts relating to Church of England parsonage houses are
excluded, for the same reason as under the regulated tenancy
code.[23]

Finally, there appears to be no exclusion of assured tenancies
from section 19. This could lead to an inconvenient overlap of two
incompatible jurisdictions where an assured tenancy also satisfies
the section 19 definition.[24]

Examples of Restricted Contracts

(i) Tenancies granted by resident landlords

Since the Rent Act 1974, tenancies granted by resident landlords have replaced furnished tenancies as the most significant
category of restricted contracts. It is not necessary that the section
19 definition should be satisfied, as section 20 provides that so long
as a tenancy is precluded from being a protected tenancy by virtue
only of section 12 (resident landlords), it shall be treated as a
restricted contract notwithstanding that the rent may not include
payment for the use of furniture or for services.

(ii) Tenancies where "living accommodation" is shared with the landlord

As explained in Chapter 2,[25] the tenant's degree of protection in
cases where part of the accommodation is shared depends on the
person with whom it is shared, and the type of accommodation.
Briefly, the position is that the tenant is fully protected if the
accommodation in question is shared with other tenants, whether
or not it is "living accommodation." Prior to the Rent Act 1974, if
any accommodation was shared with the landlord, the tenant was

---

[21] *Ibid.* s.143, *ante* p. 34.
[22] *Ibid.* s.144. Any such order may contain transitional provisions.
[23] *Ante*, p. 33; Pettit, *Private Sector Tenancies* (2nd ed.), p. 111.
[24] See Farrand and Arden, *Rent Acts and Regulations* (2nd ed.), p. 55.
[25] *Ante*, p. 18.

fully protected only if the shared accommodation was not "living accommodation." The expression "living accommodation" covers rooms such as kitchens and sitting rooms, but not halls and bathrooms.[26] Where a tenant is sharing rooms with his landlord, the landlord will normally be resident, and the "sharing" rules have accordingly been largely superseded by the resident landlord provisions, introduced by the Rent Act 1974. The latter provisions, however, have no application to unfurnished tenancies granted before the 1974 Act.[27] In such a case the "sharing" rules still apply, hence an unfurnished tenancy, granted before the 1974 Act, under which the tenant shares "living accommodation" with the landlord, is not a protected tenancy. Instead, it has the status of a restricted contract. This is so even if the rent does not include payment for the use of furniture or for services.[28]

(iii) Contractual licences

Unlike the other provisions of the Rent Act 1977, the restricted contract code embraces not only tenancies but also certain licences. This is the result of the definition in section 19(2), which requires a contract rather than a letting, and of the extended definition of "lessee" and "lessor" in section 19(8).[29]

For a licence to be a restricted contract,

   (a) it must be in consideration of a rent;

   (b) the rent must include payment for the use of furniture or for services;

   (c) it must grant the right to occupy dwelling as a residence[30];

   (d) the grantee must be entitled to exclusive occupation[31]; and

   (e) it must not be excluded by any of the express provisions discussed in the previous section of this chapter.

Several of these requirements were explained in the leading case of *Luganda* v. *Service Hotels Ltd.*,[32] where the plaintiff had lived

---

[26] *Ante*, p. 18.
[27] See now R.A. 1977, Sched. 24, para. 6.
[28] R.A. 1977, s.21.
[29] *Ante*, p. 107.
[30] A company, therefore, could not qualify, as it is incapable of "residing." This is established by the statutory tenancy cases, *ante*, p. 55.
[31] s.19(6), *ante*, p. 107.
[32] [1969] 2 Ch. 209. See also *Marchant* v. *Charters* [1977] 1 W.L.R. 1181, *infra*; *R.* v. *South Middlesex Rent Tribunal, ex p. Beswick* (1976) 32 P. & C.R. 67 (Y.W.C.A.).

for three years in a residential hotel as licensee of a bed-sitting room. He cooked his own meals, but the hotel provided bedding, and chambermaids cleaned the rooms daily and changed the linen weekly. After a dispute resulting from a rent increase the locks were changed, but the plaintiff successfully sought an injunction to reinstate him. He had the benefit of a restricted contract, and the eviction was accordingly unlawful. While a hotel guest, for example at the Ritz,[33] would not normally succeed in establishing a restricted contract, the plaintiff was here to be regarded as occupying the dwelling as a residence. There is no necessity that the contract should expressly confer a right to "reside." It is sufficient that the licensee is within his rights to occupy the property as a residence. The plaintiff also satisfied the requirement of exclusive occupation, which signifies something less than exclusive possession. A lodger has exclusive occupation of his room, although the landlady has a right of access at all times; she does not have the right to occupy the room herself or to put someone else in. As Lord Denning M.R. explained, "A person has a right to 'exclusive occupation' of a room when he is entitled to occupy it himself, and no-one else is entitled to occupy it."[34]

This requirement of exclusive occupation led to the common practice, upheld by the Court of Appeal in *Somma* v. *Hazelhurst*,[35] of the sharing device, whereby the occupant agreed to share the accommodation with one or more others in such manner that none of them, it was held, had exclusive occupation. In this way the occupants were denied even the limited protection of the restricted contract code. This decision, as we have seen, was regarded as incorrect by the House of Lords in *Street* v. *Mountford*.[36] The latter decision is of great significance in the present context. First, by enabling the sharing device to be disregarded as a sham, it brings the occupiers in such cases into the restricted contract régime, as they can now establish (joint) exclusive occupation. Secondly, and more fundamentally, the decision enables certain occupiers who might previously have been regarded as licensees to establish a tenancy, thus bringing themselves into full protection, as in the case of *Street* v. *Mountford* itself. It is only those occupiers regarded by the House of Lords as genuine licensees, such as lodgers, who will remain within the limited protection of the restricted contract régime. Licensees will only be outside the

[33] See the example in Megarry's *Rent Acts* (10th ed.), p. 505, approved by Lord Denning M.R. in *Luganda*.
[34] [1969] 2 Ch. 209 at 219.
[35] [1978] 1 W.L.R. 1014, *ante*, p. 9.
[36] [1985] A.C. 809, *ante*, p. 10.

Act altogether by reason of the exclusive occupation requirement where there is a genuine sharing arrangement, as where, for example, a person shares a room in a hostel with other independent occupiers whose identities change from time to time.

(iv) Furnished student lettings or licences

Unlike the regulated tenancy code, there is no exclusion of student lettings from section 19. Provided the requirements of section 19(2) as to furniture or services are satisfied, there is no reason why such arrangements should not constitute restricted contracts. It is unlikely however, that the occupation of Halls of Residence, could be so regarded. Assuming that the Hall could be regarded as a "house,"[37] and that the occupants would be able to establish exclusive occupation, they are likely to be excluded by the "board" rule.

(v) Tenancies with board which is less than substantial

We have seen that a tenancy cannot be regulated if there is any element of board (which is more than *de minimis*), and that section 19(5) excludes from the restricted contract régime any contract for letting at a rent which includes payments for board, where the payments form a substantial proportion of the rent. Hence a restricted contract will come into being where the payments for board are less than substantial.

(vi) Tenancies with substantial attendance

A licence can qualify as a restricted contract where the rent includes payments for attendance, whether or not substantial. A tenancy on the other hand, will be regulated in spite of attendance provided the latter is not substantial.[38] It will, accordingly, be a restricted contract where the attendance is substantial.

In *Marchant* v. *Charters*[39] the occupant lived in a furnished bedsitting room equipped with cooking facilities. A resident housekeeper cleaned the rooms daily and provided clean linen weekly. If there had been a tenancy it would have been a restricted contract rather than a protected tenancy because the services mentioned above amounted to substantial attendance. However, the occupant was held to be only a contractual licensee. Thus the

---

[37] R.A. 1977, s.19(8); *Luganda* v. *Service Hotels Ltd., supra.*
[38] *Ibid.* s.7(2), *ante*, p. 25.
[39] [1977] 1 W.L.R. 1181, *ante*, p. 26.

restricted contract code applied, irrespective of the degree of attendance.

Security of Tenure

A distinction must be drawn between restricted contracts entered into before and after the amendments in the Housing Act 1980 took effect. The concepts of the statutory tenancy and succession rights have never been applicable to restricted contracts. Prior to the 1980 Act, however, limited security of tenure was conferred on certain restricted contracts. This has effectively been removed by the 1980 Act.

(i) Contracts entered into before November 28, 1980

The position differs according to whether the restricted contract is for a fixed term or is terminable by notice to quit.[40] In the former case, there is no security of tenure, while in the latter case, there is. This is because security takes the form of postponing the operation of a notice to quit, which cannot apply to a fixed term.

The object of the security provisions prior to the 1980 Act was that a tenant should be able to refer his rent to the rent tribunal without fear of retaliation by the landlord in the form of an effective notice to quit.

The first situation to consider is where the tenant[41] refers his rent to the rent tribunal before any notice to quit has been served. By section 103 of the 1977 Act, a notice to quit served subsequently, either before the tribunal's decision or within six months thereafter, cannot take effect before the expiry of the six-month period. By section 103(2), the rent tribunal may direct a shorter period than six months if it thinks fit. If the reference to the rent tribunal is withdrawn, the period during which the notice to quit cannot take effect is seven days from the withdrawal of the reference. The period of six months mentioned above may be extended by further applications under section 104, discussed below.

The second situation is where a notice to quit has already been served. If it has actually expired, the rent tribunal has no jurisdiction. If, however, it has not yet taken effect, the tenant (or licensee) may apply to the rent tribunal under section 104 for an

---

[40] It seems that contractual licences may be included here, although not terminable by notice to quit in the technical sense; see *Luganda* v. *Service Hotels Ltd., supra.*

[41] Or the local authority; R.A. 1977, ss.77, 80.

extension of the period of the notice to quit. In such a case the notice to quit cannot take effect before the determination of the application unless the application is withdrawn. Section 104 applies either where the notice to quit has not yet taken effect under the general law or where it is being prolonged under section 103 above. Where the tenant applies under section 104, the rent tribunal must make such inquiries as it thinks fit and must give each party an opportunity of being heard or of submitting written representations. It may then direct that the notice to quit shall not have effect until the end of a specified period not exceeding six months from the date the notice would have taken effect apart from the direction.[42] If the rent tribunal refuses to give such a direction, the notice to quit cannot take effect before the expiry of seven days from the determination of the application. In such a case no futher application may be made in respect of the same notice to quit.[43]

In theory the tenant can make an infinite number of applications under section 104. In practice, rent tribunals:

> "appear to be primarily influenced by the parties' conduct, looking for the fault causing any breakdown of the landlord and tenant relationship. Subject to this, the reasonable needs of the lessor, personal and financial, will be balanced against the availability of alternative accommodation of any sort for the lessee."[44]

During any period of suspension under either section 103 or section 104, the landlord may refer back to the rent tribunal for a reduction of the period of suspension. This may be done under section 106, on the ground that the lessee has not complied with the terms of the contract; or that the lessee (or any person residing or lodging with him) has been guilty of conduct which is a nuisance or annoyance to adjoining occupiers or has been convicted of using the dwelling, or allowing the dwelling to be used, for an immoral or illegal purpose[45]; or that the condition of the dwelling has deteriorated owing to any act or neglect of the lessee (or any person residing or lodging with him); or that the condition of any furniture has deteriorated owing to ill-treatment by the lessee (or any person residing or lodging with him). In such cases the rent tri-

---

[42] R.A. 1977, s.104(3).
[43] *Ibid.* s.104(4).
[44] Farrand and Arden, *Rent Acts and Regulations* (2nd ed.), pp. 134–135.
[45] See the similar provisions of Case 2 in respect of regulated tenancies, *ante*, p. 75.

bunal may reduce the period of suspension of the notice to quit so as to end at a date specified in the direction. Then the lessee may make no further application under section 104.[46]

Finally, section 105 provides an "owner-occupier" ground similar to Case 11, which, as we have seen, gives a mandatory ground for possession in respect of regulated tenancies.[47] This is unlikely to be much used today, as it relates to non-resident landlords, hence the occupier is more likely to have a regulated tenancy than a restricted contract. It might, however, have some scope in relation to licences, although even in that case it will not be necessary to invoke it if the licence is for a fixed period, and therefore outside the security provisions.

(ii) Contracts entered into after November 28, 1980[48]

Section 69 of the Housing Act 1980 has reduced the security provisions outlined above, but has also ended the artificial distinction between fixed term and periodic restricted contracts.

Section 106A of the 1977 Act, introduced by section 69 of the 1980 Act, provides that on the making of a possession order, or at any time before its execution, the court may stay or suspend execution of the order or postpone the date of possession for no longer than three months after the making of the order. This is the maximum period; it cannot be prolonged by further applications.

On any such stay, suspension or postponement, the court shall, unless it considers that to do so would cause exceptional hardship to the lessee or would otherwise be unreasonable, impose conditions with regard to the payment of rent or mesne profits and any arrears and may impose such other conditions as it thinks fit.[49]

As the mechanism of this new scheme is the suspension of a possession order, it is essential that the lessor be obliged to obtain such an order. A court order was already required in the case of tenants, whether fixed or periodic,[50] but was not normally required in the case of licensees. In order to bring licensees within

---

[46] The county court may reduce the period of suspension on similar grounds if the lessor brings possession proceedings during the period of suspension; R.A. 1977, s.106(4).

[47] *Ante*, p. 82.

[48] It seems that neither set of rules applies to a contract entered into *on* November 28, 1980.

[49] R.A. 1977, s.106A(4). See also s.106A(5) and (6), giving the same rights in relation to any stay, suspension or postponement to the lessee's spouse having rights of occupation under the Matrimonial Homes Act (now the Act of 1983).

[50] Protection from Eviction Act 1977, s.3, *ante*, p. 7.

the new scheme, the Housing Act 1980 provides that licensees cannot be evicted without a court order where the licence is a restricted contract entered into after November 28, 1980.[51] Thus the new scheme applies to all restricted contracts, whether fixed term tenancies, periodic tenancies, or licences.

It will be appreciated that the effect of the current provisions, unlike those operating prior to the Housing Act 1980, is that a landlord can now respond to a tenant's applications to the rent tribunal for a rent reduction by an effective notice to quit. The limited suspension powers outlined above cannot be compared with the theoretically indefinite security afforded by the 1977 Act.

Rent Control

Only an outline will be given here, as the matter will be more fully discussed in Chapter 10.

Where there is no registered rent, there is no restriction on the rent payable under a restricted contract, nor does the prohibition on premiums apply.[52]

Either party to the restricted contract or the local authority can refer the contract to the rent tribunal.[53] Provided the reference is not withdrawn, the rent tribunal must consider it. After giving the parties an opportunity to be heard or to make written representations, the tribunal must either approve the rent, reduce or increase it to such sum as they think reasonable in all the circumstances, or dismiss the reference.[54] Thus the concept of the "fair rent," applicable to regulated tenancies,[55] does not apply here, although no criteria are laid down by which a "reasonable rent" may be distinguished from a "fair rent." Where the rent is increased, the increase takes effect immediately.[56] The rent as approved, reduced or increased by the rent tribunal is to be registered.[57] Once registered, the parties or the local authority may

---

[51] H.A. 1980, s.69(1), amending s.3 of the Protection from Eviction Act 1977.

[52] *Post,* p. 157. This is so even where there is a registered rent relating to the whole premises, provided only part is being let.

[53] R.A. 1977, s.77. The rent tribunal is now the same body as a rent assessment committee, being called a rent tribunal when exercising its jurisdiction in relation to restricted contracts; H.A. 1980, s.72.

[54] R.A. 1977, s.78.

[55] *Post,* p. 134.

[56] *Villa D'Este Restaurant Ltd.* v. *Burton* [1957] 2 Q.B. 214. It can even precede the date of registration. By s.78(4), the approval, reduction or increase may be limited to a particular period.

[57] R.A. 1977, s.79.

refer to the rent tribunal for a reconsideration of the rent,[58] but, save in the case where the parties apply jointly, the tribunal shall not be required to entertain the reference within two years from the previous consideration of the rent unless the registered rent is no longer reasonable, in view of a change in the condition of the dwelling, the furniture or services, the terms of the contract, or any other circumstances taken into account when the rent was last considered.[59] Section 71 of the Housing Act 1980 permits a registered rent to be cancelled after two years where the dwelling is not presently subject to a restricted contract, on the application of the person who would be the lessor if there were such a contract. The lessor may then enter into a new restricted contract at a higher rent, but this is without prejudice to a further registration. In the absence of cancellation, the registration operates *in rem*, and affects future restricted contracts.

Where there is a registered rent, it is unlawful to require or receive a higher rent, any excess being recoverable by the lessee.[60]

The rent tribunal only has the above jurisdiction where the contract is indeed a restricted contract. Where it is alleged that it is not, the tribunal must decide whether it has jurisdiction. If it so decides, it will then proceed with the matter, but the parties may have the question of jurisdiction resolved by the county court.[61]

---

[58] *Ibid.* s.80(1).
[59] *Ibid.* s.80(2), as amended by H.A. 1980, s.70.
[60] R.A. 1977, s.81. The penalty is a fine and/or imprisonment. Proceedings may be instituted by the local authority. Apparently they are rarely brought.
[61] R.A. 1977, s.141.

Chapter 9

SUB-TENANTS

It is clear that the Rent Act applies between tenant and sub-tenant in exactly the same way as between landlord and tenant.[1] The question to be considered here, however, is the extent to which a sub-tenant, who is protected by the Rent Act as against the tenant, has any rights against the head landlord upon the determination of the mesne tenancy.

Sub-tenants have certain rights against the head landlord under the general law. These rights, mentioned below, may be relied on in addition to any Rent Act rights. In the absence of any general law rights, the sub-tenant must look to the Rent Act alone for his protection.

The general rule at common law is that a sub-tenancy cannot survive after the termination of the tenancy from which it derives, for "every subordinate interest must perish with the superior interest on which it is dependent."[2] To this rule there are several exceptions. So, for example, where a tenancy ends by forfeiture, a sub-tenant may become tenant of the head landlord if he is granted relief from forfeiture by the court.[3] If a tenancy ends by merger or surrender, the sub-tenant's rights are preserved by statute.[4] Similarly in the case of disclaimer of the tenancy.[5] Thus the sub-tenant may invoke these rights, where applicable, whether or not he is within the Rent Act. Section 137 of the Rent Act 1977, discussed below, provides a further exception to the common law rule. If, however, the sub-tenant cannot bring himself within the requirements of that section, he will have no rights against the landlord on the determination of the tenancy,[6] save to the extent that the limited exceptions under the general law can be relied on.

Before considering section 137, mention might briefly be made of the extent to which other codes of statutory protection confer rights on sub-tenants beyond those existing under the general law.

---

[1] See the definitions of "let" and "tenancy" in R.A. 1977, s.152(1).
[2] *Bendall* v. *McWhirter* [1952] 2 Q.B. 466 at 487.
[3] Law of Property Act 1925, s.146(4).
[4] *Ibid.* s.139. Likewise if the tenant gives notice to quit; *Mellor* v. *Watkins* (1874) L.R. Q.B. 400 at 404.
[5] *Re Thompson & Cottrell's Contract* [1943] Ch. 97.
[6] *Cf. Jessamine Investment Co.* v. *Schwartz* [1978] Q.B. 264, *post*, p. 130.

At one end of the spectrum, full statutory rights against superior landlords exist in the case of business sub-tenancies[7] and long residential sub-tenancies, in the latter case both as to security of tenure[8] and enfranchisement.[9] At the other end, sub-tenants have no rights under the agricultural holdings legislation.[10] In the middle is the Rent Act régime, under which sub-tenants have some rights against the landlord, but certainly not full rights. The point is unlikely to arise in the public sector, where a secure tenancy ceases to be secure if the whole is sublet.[11] Thus no uniformity of treatment can be discerned in the various statutory schemes.

Section 137

A distinction is drawn between cases where the tenant (*i.e.* the sub-tenant's immediate landlord) is himself a Rent Act tenant and where he is not. These situations will be considered in turn.

(i) Sub-tenant of a Rent Act tenant

By section 137(1), if a court makes an order for possession of a dwelling-house from a protected or statutory tenant,[12] and the order is made by virtue of section 98(1)[13] (the discretionary grounds), nothing in the order shall affect the right of any sub-tenant to whom the dwelling-house or any part of it has been lawfully sublet before the commencement of the proceedings to retain possession by virtue of this Part (Part XI) of the Act, nor shall the order operate to give a right to possession against any such sub-tenant.

This provision, which will be explained in detail below, applies to protect a sub-tenant of a Rent Act tenant when possession is recovered from the latter on the basis of one of the discretionary

---

[7] L.T.A. 1954, s.44.
[8] *Ibid.* s.21. (R.A. 1977, s.137(5), confers certain rights on Rent Act subtenants on termination of a superior long tenancy; *post,* p. 121.)
[9] Leasehold Reform Act 1967, Sched. 1.
[10] *Sherwood* v. *Moody* [1952] 1 All E.R. 389. But see A.H.A. 1984, Sched. 3, para. 9, giving compensation rights where the sub-tenancy ends by reason of the termination of the superior tenancy.
[11] H.A. 1985, s.93. A subletting of part is, however, permitted if the landlord gives written consent; *ibid.* However, there are no provisions protecting the sub-tenant against the landlord.
[12] Or a protected occupier or statutory tenant within the Rent (Agriculture) Act 1976. This aspect will not be dealt with.
[13] *Ante,* p. 73.

grounds for possession. It does not spell out what the sub-tenant's position is, nor does it deal with cases where the tenancy terminates for other reasons. These matters fall within section 137(2), where on the termination of a statutorily protected tenancy,[14] either as a result of a possession order or for any other reason, any sub-tenant to whom the dwelling-house or any part of it has been lawfully sublet shall be deemed to become the tenant of the landlord, on the same terms as if the tenant's tenancy had continued. This sub-section would apply, for example, where a statutory tenancy terminates because the tenant ceases to reside.[15] The reason why the sub-tenant is deemed to become tenant of the landlord is so that a relationship of privity should exist between them, enabling their rights and obligations to be mutually enforceable.

Before considering in full the implication of these provisions a few preliminary points should be examined.

(a) Lawful sub-tenant

Both subsections (1) and (2) of section 137 are confined to the case where the dwelling has been "lawfully sublet." Thus an unlawful sub-tenant has no rights under the Act as against the head landlord.[16] He can only invoke the exceptions to the common law rule (where relevant) if the tenancy was still protected, as a statutory tenancy cannot end by the methods envisaged by those exceptions, such as forfeiture.

What is meant by a lawful sub-tenant? Where the sub-letting was in breach of a prohibition in the tenancy, the dwelling will not be "lawfully sublet" unless the breach has been waived. Thus in *Metropolitan Property Co. Ltd.* v. *Cordery*[17] waiver was established where the landlord's agents knew that the sub-tenant was in residence (the sub-tenant having lived openly in the premises for some years). This knowledge was imputed to the landlord, who had accordingly waived the breach by taking rent. Where, however, the subletting in breach has been done by a statutory tenant, it will be more difficult to establish waiver, as the strict common

---

[14] Defined by s.137(4) as meaning a protected statutory tenancy (or a protected occupancy or statutory tenancy within the Rent (Agriculture) Act 1976, or, in certain cases, a tenancy of an agricultural holding). By s.137(5), a long tenancy at a low rent is treated as a statutorily protected tenancy for the purpose of s.137(2) if it would have been a protected tenancy but for the low rent.

[15] *Ante*, p. 55.

[16] Unless by analogy with *Jessamine Investment Co.* v. *Schwartz* [1978] Q.B. 264, *post*, p. 130; (1978) 41 Conv. (N.S.) 96 at 104 (J. Martin).

[17] (1980) 39 P. & C.R. 10.

law rules do not apply. A mere demand for rent with knowledge of the breach does not inevitably amount to waiver in such circumstances.[18] If the tenancy permits subletting of a particular type only, then a subletting outside the terms specified will be unlawful.[19] Likewise, if the tenancy, while not expressly prohibiting subletting, contains a covenant to use the property as a single dwelling-house only.

We have seen that one of the discretionary grounds for possession, Case 6, involves the situation where, without the consent of the landlord, the tenant has sublet the whole of the dwelling-house or sublet part of it, the remainder being already sublet.[20] If such a subletting was in breach of the terms of the tenancy, then it will be unlawful, as discussed above. It is established, however, that Case 6 applies also to sublettings which did not constitute a breach of the terms of the tenancy. In *Leith Properties Ltd.* v. *Byrne*,[21] where there was no covenant against subletting, the landlord invoked Case 6 where the tenant had sublet without consent, seeking possession against the tenant and the sub-tenant. One argument was that the subletting must be considered unlawful as it was within the terms of Case 6. This argument was rejected. The fact that a subletting gives rise to a ground for possession under Case 6 does not make it unlawful for the purpose of section 137. The landlord was, however, entitled to possession, for reasons explained below.

Finally, where a subletting is unlawful and accordingly outside the protection of section 137, it seems that it is also outside the protection of section 3 of the Protection from Eviction Act 1977[22] (requiring a court order for possession) because that section applies only where the tenancy is *not* "statutorily protected." As indicated above, section 137(1) and (2) apply only where the tenancy is so protected.

---

[18] *Oak Property Co. Ltd.* v. *Chapman* [1947] K.B. 886 (qualified demand); *Trustees of Henry Smith's Charity* v. *Willson* [1983] Q.B. 316 (unqualified demand).

[19] *Trustees of Henry Smith's Charity* v. *Willson, supra* (Covenant against subletting without consent save in respect of a term not exceeding six months); *Patoner Ltd.* v. *Lowe* (1985) 275 E.G. 540 (Tenancy permitted subletting "consistent with the letting of high-class furnished accommodation." Sub-tenancy unlawful where second-hand furniture, no table and substandard armchairs).

[20] *Ante*, p. 77.

[21] [1983] Q.B. 433 (*sub nom. Leith Properties Ltd.* v. *Springer* in [1982] 3 All E.R. 731).

[22] *Ante*, p. 7.

(*b*) *Must the sub-tenant himself be a protected or statutory tenant?*

It is clear that the head tenancy must be a protected or statutory tenancy (and not, for example, a restricted contract) if section 137(1) and (2) are to apply. It is less clear whether the sub-tenancy itself must be protected or statutory. The wording of these provisions may be contrasted with that of section 137(3) (discussed below), where it is expressly stated that the sub-tenancy must be protected or statutory. Section 137(1), as we have seen, permits the sub-tenant "to retain possession by virtue of this Part of this Act" when the head tenancy is terminated by a possession order. Subsection (2) provides that he shall, "subject to this Act," be deemed to become tenant of the landlord. It is clear that the sub-tenancy must fall within the Rent Act. The problem is whether it is sufficient that it be a restricted contract instead of a protected or statutory tenancy. It is submitted that this is not sufficient.[23] As the sub-tenant who falls within the section has, by section 137(2), the same rights against the head landlord as he had against the former tenant, it is difficult to envisage how this provision could operate in the case of a restricted contract. The usual reason why the sub-tenant has a restricted contract is because the tenant (his immediate landlord) is resident. On termination of the tenant's interest, there would be difficulties in applying the restricted contract rules against the head landlord, who is not resident.[24]

It has been pointed out that the difficulty has been compounded by a draftman's error in the consolidating provisions of the 1977 Act.[25] It is clear that under previous legislation the sub-tenant was only within the equivalent provision if he was protected or statutory.[26] Section 137(1) refers to the sub-tenant's right to retain possession by "this Part of the Act." This refers to Part XI, which contains no provisions on security of tenure, and is, therefore, an error. The identical words in section 18 of the 1968 Act were contained in a Part conferring security of tenure for protected and statutory tenancies, but which did not deal with restricted contracts. It is suggested that the position should be regarded as simi-

---

[23] A contrary assumption is made in Yates and Hawkins, *Landlord and Tenant Law,* p. 348. See also Evans, *The Law of Landlord and Tenant* (2nd ed.), pp. 305, 306.

[24] Under the resident landlord rules (*ante,* Chap. 3), a tenant becomes fully protected if the landlord ceases to reside. To apply that rule here would infringe the principle of s.137(2) that the sub-tenant has the same status against the landlord as if the tenancy continued.

[25] See Farrand and Arden, *Rent Acts and Regulations* (2nd ed.), p. 158. See also Pettit, *Private Sector Tenancies* (2nd ed.), p. 277.

[26] See *Stanley* v. *Compton* [1951] 1 All E.R. 859.

lar under the 1977 Act, so that sub–tenants having restricted contracts are not within the protection of section 137. This view is supported by the wording of section 138, discussed below. Upon this assumption, section 137 will only apply to sublettings of part of a dwelling if the tenant did not reside in the remainder.

(c) *Can a statutory tenant sublet the whole of the dwelling?*

Clearly a protected tenant can effectively sublet the whole or part of the property at common law, so as to confer an estate on the sub-tenant. (Of course, any such subletting will be unlawful if in breach of a prohibition in the tenancy). Although a statutory tenant has no "estate" out of which to grant a sub-tenancy, it has long been accepted that he can effectively sublet part.[27] Doubts have been expressed, however, as to whether a statutory tenant can effectively sublet the whole.[28] It has even been suggested that such a subletting would be "unlawful" (and, therefore, outside the scope of section 137).[29] The problem is that a statutory tenant, by the act of subletting the whole, goes out of residence and thereupon ceases to satisfy the requirements of section 2 of the 1977 Act.[30] His interest, therefore, terminates,[31] giving rise to conceptual difficulties in treating a sub-tenant as deriving a valid title from the statutory tenant who loses his status by the very act of subletting.

Section 137 and Case 6 of Schedule 15 clearly refer to subletting of the whole or part by protected or statutory tenants, but do not conclusively answer the point. They could for example, refer to the situation where the statutory tenant intends to return and, accordingly, does not lose his interest.[32]

The matter was touched upon in *Leith Properties Ltd.* v. *Byrne*,[33] but left open, as the subletting there occurred while the tenancy was contractual. It arose also in *Trustees of Henry Smith's Charity* v. *Willson*,[34] where a statutory tenant sublet the whole. In fact the subletting was unlawful, so that section 137 did not apply

[27] *Roe* v. *Russell* [1928] 2 K.B. 117.
[28] Megarry, *The Rent Acts* (10th ed.), p. 455; Evans *The Law of Landlord and Tenant* (2nd ed.), p. 305.
[29] *Roe* v. *Russell, supra,* pp. 130, 141. The point was left open in *Keeves* v. *Dean* [1924] 1 K.B. 685 and *Oak Property Co. Ltd.* v. *Chapman* [1947] K.B. 886.
[30] *Ante,* p. 55.
[31] Unless the subletting is temporary and he intends to return; Pettit, *Private Sector Tenancies* (2nd ed.), p. 76.
[32] See [1983] Conv. 248 at 249–250 (J. Martin).
[33] [1983] Q.B. 433.
[34] [1983] Q.B. 316; [1983] Conv. 248 (J. Martin).

for that reason. The Court of Appeal, however, discussed the issue. Slade L.J. felt that the statutory provisions indicated the possibility of a subletting of the whole by a statutory tenant, but did not attempt to "grapple further with the conceptual problems." Ormrod L.J. however, was more firmly of the view that such a subletting was possible. The Act clearly contemplated it, and it was a mistake to try to impress common law concepts on to the legal relationships created by the Rent Act, from which the incidents of the statutory tenancy must be collected.

In conclusion, it appears that a subletting of the whole by a statutory tenant is not without effect. If the act of subletting causes the statutory tenancy to cease,[35] then the tenant loses his rights automatically (*i.e.* it is not necessary to invoke Case 6, a discretionary ground, against him). In such a case the sub-tenant, provided the subletting was not unlawful, will be within section 137. However, as explained below, the sub-tenant remains vulnerable to any ground for possession, such as Case 6 itself, which may be invoked against him.

Having considered these preliminary matters, let us now examine the precise effect of the provisions of section 137(1) and (2). A first reading of these provisions may give the impression that a subtenant is not prejudiced by the termination of the tenancy, and that he continues to enjoy security of tenure against the head landlord. The authorities indicate that the protection of these provisions is extremely limited.

In *Leith Properties Ltd.* v. *Byrne*[36] a protected quarterly tenant sublet the whole property on a weekly tenancy. This was done without the landlord's consent, but the tenancy did not prohibit subletting. After serving notice to quit, the landlord sought to recover possession from both tenant and sub-tenant under Case 6 (the discretionary ground applicable where the tenant has sublet the whole without consent). It might be noted that as the tenant had gone to Australia, not intending to return, it is difficult to see how his statutory tenancy survived until the proceedings, in which case it should not have been necessary to invoke Case 6 against him.[37] However, on the basis that the landlord did need to establish Case 6 as against the tenant, the Court of Appeal confirmed that Case 6 applied even where the subletting involved no breach, on the ground that its purpose was that the landlord should be able to recover possession where there is an assignee or sub-tenant

---

[35] *i.e.* because the tenant does not intend to return.
[36] [1983] Q.B. 433; [1983] Conv. 155 (J. Martin).
[37] On this view, the sub-tenant's rights would be governed by s.137(2).

"unknown to and not approved by the landlord." As already mentioned, the fact that Case 6 applied did not mean that the subletting was to be regarded as unlawful.[38] Although section 137
applied to the sub-tenant, it was held that the protection was not
absolute. The sub-tenant only becomes tenant of the landlord
"subject to this Act," and under the Act the landlord could
recover possession from him under Case 6, where the words "the
tenant" referred to the mesne tenant. Hence a subletting by him
gave a ground for possession against the sub-tenant also, notwithstanding that the latter had not assigned or sublet without consent.
It was said that, on any other construction, Case 6 would be use-
less and its purpose defeated. The case was remitted to determine
whether it was reasonable to order possession against the sub-
tenant.

Thus the protection of section 137 will often be more apparent
than real. The sub-tenant is not entitled to stay in possession without regard to anything the tenant has done. His protection is two-
fold: first, a possession order obtained against the tenant alone
does not affect him (in other words, he must be made a party to
the proceedings); secondly, the issue of reasonableness (in the
context of the discretionary grounds) must be decided as between
landlord and sub-tenant and not merely as between landlord and
tenant. The substance of the matter, however, is that the ground
invoked against the tenant may also be invoked against the sub-
tenant: it is not necessary for the landlord to find a new ground
against the latter. It might be added that, as far as Case 6 is concerned, the fact that the subletting was not in breach of the
tenancy might make the court less inclined to find it reasonable to
make the possession order.[39]

It remains to consider how far this construction of Case 6 applies
to other grounds for possession. It was said that in "some contexts" the word "tenant" as it appears in the discretionary grounds
means the last immediate tenant of the landlord. A similar view of
Case 5 (tenant's notice to quit) was taken in *Lord Hylton* v.
Heal,[40] to the effect that the ground would be available also
against the sub-tenant, even though *he* had given no notice to quit.
It was also suggested in that case that Case 1 (unpaid rent or other

---

[38] Distinguishing *Roe* v. *Russell* [1928] 2 K.B. 117, where it was suggested
that a subletting of the whole by a statutory tenant would be unlawful;
cf. *Trustees of Henry Smith's Charity* v. *Willson, supra.*

[39] *Trustees of Henry Smith's Charity* v. *Willson, supra,* where, however, it
was said that the fact of a breach would only make the court marginally
more inclined to make the order.

[40] [1921] 2 K.B. 438.

breach), Case 2 (nuisance or annoyance) and Case 8 (tenant was landlord's employee and employment has ceased) should be similarly construed. This seems hard on the sub-tenant. If these views are correct, there is hardly a ground which will not be available against the sub-tenant as well as the tenant. Case 10 (tenant charging sub-tenant an excessive rent) cannot be distinguished on its wording from the above-mentioned grounds, but it seems harsh that it should operate against the sub-tenant. It is submitted that Case 10 and Cases 1 to 4 should not be available against the sub-tenant if he himself has not done the act complained of. Otherwise there is indeed little substance in the protection of section 137. However, as the issue of reasonableness must be decided independently as between the landlord and sub-tenant, it may well be that, assuming these grounds are available against the sub-tenant, the court may not consider it reasonable to grant possession against him where the act complained of is that of the tenant.

The position may be contrasted with that under section 137(3), discussed below, where the sub-tenant will fare better. That subsection applies where the mesne tenancy is not a Rent Act tenancy. In such a case the tenancy cannot terminate by a Rent Act ground for possession. Hence the landlord can only recover possession from the sub-tenant by establishing a ground against him personally.

The position may also differ where the statutory tenancy has already terminated (for example, because the tenant has ceased to reside), so that it will not be necessary to invoke a ground for possession against the tenant. In such a case the sub-tenant will have become tenant under section 137(2), and it would seem that the landlord must establish a ground against him directly.[41] It is difficult to see how an act done in the past by a person who is no longer the tenant at the date of the proceedings should be a ground for possession against the present tenant.

Finally, where the tenant is a shorthold tenant,[42] it is expressly provided that where the whole or part of the property has been sublet,[43] section 137 shall not apply if the landlord becomes entitled to possession as against the tenant.[44] Hence he becomes entitled to possession as against the sub-tenant also.

---

[41] See Pettit, *Private Sector Tenancies* (2nd ed.), p. 274.
[42] *Ante,* Chap. 4.
[43] During the "continuous period" specified in H.A. 1980, s.54(3), *ante,* p. 49.
[44] H.A. 1980, s.54(1). It is not clear whether this provision abrogates any common law rights the sub-tenant may have, as where, for example, the shorthold tenancy ends by surrender or tenant's notice to quit.

(ii) Sub-tenant of a non Rent Act tenant

The provisions discussed above do not apply unless the mesne tenant is a protected or statutory tenant. If he is not, the relevant provision is section 137(3). Where a dwelling-house forms part of "premises" which have been let as a whole on a superior tenancy which is not a statutorily protected tenancy, but the sub-tenancy itself is protected or statutory, then,

> "from the coming to an end of the superior tenancy, this Act shall apply in relation to the dwelling-house as if, in lieu of the superior tenancy, there had been separate tenancies of the dwelling-house and of the remainder of the premises, for the like purposes as under the superior tenancy, and at rents equal to the just proportion of the rent under the superior tenancy."

The circumstances envisaged here are that there is a subletting of part to a sub-tenant who is within the Rent Act as against the tenant, but the tenant is not a protected or statutory tenant himself, because, for example, the superior tenancy exceeds the rateable value limits, while the sublet part does not; or because the superior tenancy is a business tenancy while the sublet part is residential (*e.g.* a head lease of a shop with a flat above, the latter being sublet); or, perhaps, because the head tenancy is excluded from the Rent Act by section 6,[45] because, although it includes a dwelling-house (which is sublet), this is ancillary to some non-residential purpose.

Section 137(3) is somewhat obscure. Its effect is not that there is deemed to be a notional lease of the sublet part direct to the sub-tenant, but that there are deemed to be two notional head leases, of the sublet part and of the remainder, so that if the notional head lease of the sublet part would have been protected, the sub-tenant may rely on section 137(2) on its determination.[46] The subsection is, therefore, subsidiary to section 137(2). It does not apply where the subletting is of the whole of the premises, presumably because in the circumstances envisaged, such a subletting is unlikely itself to be within the Rent Act.

It seems that section 137(3) applies only where the superior letting was residential, at least as far as the sublet part was con-

---

[45] *Ante,* p. 24.
[46] *Cadogan (Earl)* v. *Henthorne* [1957] 1 W.L.R. 1 (on the equivalent provisions of previous legislation). A consequence of this is that s.137(3) is confined to lawful sub-tenants.

cerned. In *Maunsell* v. *Olins*[47] the question was whether a pro-tected sub-tenant of a cottage on a farm could invoke the subsec-tion on the termination of the head tenancy, which was an agricultural holding. The House of Lords held, by a majority, that he could not. The word "premises" in subsection (3) was limited to dwelling-houses and did not apply to a farm.[48] Lord Reid, who found the section "unusually difficult,"[49] held that section 137(3) applied only if the head lease was residential or had two purposes, one of which was residential. In the present case it had only one purpose, which was agricultural.

This decision was partly reversed by the Rent (Agriculture) Act 1976.[50] It is now provided that "premises" in section 137(3) includes an agricultural holding within the meaning of the Agricul-tural Holdings Act 1948. Thus residential sub-tenants of agricul-tural tenants may be protected by s.137(3).[51] The construction adopted in *Maunsell* v. *Olins*[52] will continue to apply to cases out-side the scope of the amendment.

Furnished Sub-tenants

The passing of the Rent Act 1974, bringing furnished tenants into protection, gave rise to a need to modify the provisions of section 137 in order to deal with the situation where the tenancy was unfurnished and the sub-tenancy was furnished. Without any new provision, landlords in such circumstances would be subject to additional obligations, as the sub-tenant's rights in respect of the furniture would become directly enforceable against the landlord under section 137(2).

The present provision is section 138 of the 1977 Act. In cases where section 137(2) applies, the terms on which the sub-tenant is deemed to become tenant of the landlord shall not include any terms as to the provision by the landlord of furniture or services if the following three conditions are satisfied:

> (a) the head tenancy was neither a protected furnished tenancy nor a statutory furnished tenancy; and

---

[47] [1975] A.C. 373.
[48] *Cf. Bracey* v. *Read* [1963] Ch. 88 ("premises" includes bare land with no buildings in the context of L.T.A. 1954, Part II).
[49] [1975] A.C. 373 at 382. Lord Wilberforce commented that the provision did not "convey an impression of conspicuous clarity"; *ibid.* at p. 385.
[50] The amendment now appears in s.137(3) of the 1977 Act.
[51] The sub-tenancy must be a protected or statutory tenancy within s.99 of the 1977 Act (dwellings let to agricultural workers).
[52] *Supra.*

(b) the sub-tenancy was a protected furnished tenancy or a statutory furnished tenancy, and

(c) the landlord, within six weeks beginning with the termination of the head tenancy, serves notice on the sub-tenant that section 138 is to apply.

The reference to furnished tenancies in section 138 are to those where a substantial part of the rent is attributable to furniture.[53]

Section 138 leaves certain questions unanswered. It will be appreciated that the furniture has been provided by the tenant. If the landlord fails to serve the notice, so that the sub-tenant continues entitled to the provision of furniture, presumably the landlord must make new provision (or, if possible, buy the existing furniture from the tenant), as it is difficult to see why he should receive rent in respect of furniture which belongs to the former tenant. If the landlord does serve the notice, so that he need not provide furniture, presumably the tenant is entitled to remove it.

Information to Landlords

To the extent that landlords may become bound by the rights of sub-tenants, they need to know of their existence. To this end, section 139 of the 1977 Act obliges a Rent Act tenant who has sublet any part on a protected tenancy to supply written particulars to the landlord within 14 days of the subletting. The tenant is liable to a fine not exceeding £25 if he fails to supply the statement, or supplies a false statement.

The statement may provide the landlord with information which will enable him to invoke a ground for possession, such as Case 6 (subletting without consent) or Case 10 (tenant charging sub-tenant an excessive rent).

Sublettings Outside the Terms of Section 137

It would be reasonable to assume that a sub-tenant who fails to satisfy the conditions of section 137 would have no rights against the head landlord save those existing at common law. It seems that this assumption cannot be made, in the case of a statutory sub-tenancy, in view of the decision of the Court of Appeal in *Jessamine Investment Co.* v. *Schwartz*.[54] In that case a 99-year lease was

---

[53] R.A. 1977, s.152(1).
[54] [1978] Q.B. 264; (1977) 41 Conv. (N.S.) 96 (J. Martin). For further implications of this decision, see (1977) 41 Conv. (N.S.) 197 (P. Smith) and correspondence at [1978] Conv. 322–323.

granted in 1874. The lease was assigned, and the assignee granted a weekly protected sub-tenancy in 1937, which became statutory in 1939. The assignee disappeared in 1945, with the result that the sub-tenant, having paid no further rent, acquired title to the leasehold as against the assignee in 1957, under the Limitation Act 1939. When the head lease expired in 1973 the freeholder claimed possession from the sub-tenant. Having held that time could run under the Limitation Act in favour of a statutory tenant and that the statutory sub-tenancy remained in existence after 1957 as against the freeholder notwithstanding its transformation into a leasehold title as against the assignee, the Court of Appeal had to decide whether any provision of the Rent Act (then the Act of 1968) protected the sub-tenant on expiry of the lease. Although a long tenancy is deemed a protected tenancy for the purpose of section 137(2),[55] it was held that the sub-tenant could not rely on section 137(2), which contemplated a sub-tenancy binding on the tenant at the termination of the lease. That was not so here, because of its transformation under the Limitation Act into a leasehold title as against the tenant (*i.e.* the assignee). Even though section 137 did not apply, the Court of Appeal found in favour of the sub-tenant, holding that statutory sub-tenancy was a right "against all the world." This was the result of section 2, under which a statutory tenancy continues so long as the tenant resides. Reliance was placed on *Keeves* v. *Dean,*[56] where Scrutton L.J. said "I take it that he has a right as against all the world to remain in possession until he is turned out by an order of the Court. . . . " Scrutton L.J., however, was there discussing the status of a statutory tenant, not a statutory sub-tenant. The argument that section 2 could not assist where section 137 was not satisfied was rejected on the basis that there may be a "lacuna" in the latter section. Also rejected was the argument that the lack of any relationship of privity between the freeholder and the sub-tenant was fatal to the claim.[57]

This decision is, it is submitted, doubtful. It is hardly justified by the terms of section 2, which does not expressly deal with subtenancies. It is suggested that section 2 is subject to an overriding principle that a sub-tenancy cannot outlast the tenancy from which it derives unless section 137 applies. This is supported by previous decisions of the Court of Appeal and House of Lords which were

---

[55] s.137(5).
[56] [1924] 1 K.B. 685 at 694.
[57] The common law exceptions and s.137 import a relationship of privity necessary to the enforceability of the parties' rights and obligations, by providing that the sub-tenant becomes direct tenant of the landlord.

not cited.[58] It is difficult to see why section 137 should have been enacted if a statutory sub-tenant could simply rely on section 2. Section 138, discussed above, clearly contemplates that a sub-tenancy will only become binding on the landlord if section 137 applies. If the *Jessamine* decision is correct, then other categories of statutory sub-tenants who are not within section 137, even perhaps unlawful sub-tenants, could rely on section 2 to achieve the same result.

In conclusion, therefore, it is submitted that a sub-tenant can rely only on section 137 and not on section 2. The contrary view derives no support from the authorities prior to *Jessamine,* and introduces a privity problem. Section 2 is in general terms and does not specifically deal with sub-tenancies. As Lord Reid has said, in the context of the predecessor to section 137, we should construe it by applying "the 'rule' that a court, when in doubt about two constructions of a statutory provision, should lean towards that construction which involves the least alteration of the common law."[59]

---

[58] See *Maunsell* v. *Olins* [1975] A.C. 373; *Hobhouse* v. *Wall* [1963] 2 Q.B. 425; *Cow* v. *Casey* [1949] 1 K.B. 474 (reversed by what is now s.137(3); *Dudley and District Permanent Benefit Building Society* v. *Emerson* [1949] Ch. 707; (1977) 41 Conv. (N.S.) 96 at 102–104 (J. Martin).
[59] *Maunsell* v. *Olins* [1975] A.C. 373 at 383.

Chapter 10

RENT CONTROL

Regulated Tenancies

The general principle applicable to regulated tenancies is that the rent should not exceed a "fair rent." This is explained in detail below, but for the purposes of this introduction it suffices to say that the fair rent is less than the market rent because of the disregard of the scarcity element. In other words, the rent is fixed on the basis that there is no shortage of rental accommodation. A different scheme used to apply to controlled tenancies prior to their abolition by the Housing Act 1980. By that Act they were converted to regulated tenancies and thus brought within the fair rent system.

In outline, there is no obligation that a regulated tenancy should have a registered fair rent, but either party may apply to the rent officer for its assessment and registration. In examining the rules relating to the recoverable rent limits, it is necessary to distinguish protected and statutory tenancies. On the grant of a protected tenancy the parties may agree on whatever rent they choose if there is no rent registered in relation to the dwelling-house. A fair rent may subsequently be registered, which becomes the rent limit. If the contractual rent exceeds this, the excess is not recoverable from the tenant. If a rent is already registered on the grant of a tenancy, the contractual rent must not exceed the registered rent. If no rent is registered when the tenancy becomes statutory, the previous contractual rent continues until a higher rent is registered. If a rent is registered, it must not be exceeded. The rent under the statutory tenancy, if lower, may be increased to the level of the registered rent, the increase being phased. Once registered, a fair rent cannot be cancelled within two years, nor may it be altered within that period unless on the ground of a change of circumstances. We will see, in the last section of this chapter, that the rent control rules cannot be evaded by the charging of a capital sum (premium) on the grant or assignment of the tenancy.

It might be mentioned that tenants who pay the rent weekly must be provided with a rent book or similar document by their landlords.[1] This will contain information as to the tenant's rights,

---

[1] Landlord and Tenant Act 1985, ss.4–7 (replacing L.T.A. 1962).

for example in relation to rent registration and rent allowances from the local authority. Failure to provide a rent book, where required, is a criminal offence,[2] but does not prevent recovery of rent by the landlord.[3]

(i) The meaning of "fair rent"

The fair rent is determined according to section 70 of the 1977 Act, which specifies matters to be taken into account and those to be disregarded.

(a) *Matters to be taken into account*

By section 70(1), regard is to be had to all the circumstances (other than personal circumstances) and in particular to the age, character, locality and state of repair of the dwelling-house. If furniture is provided under the tenancy, its quantity, quality and condition must be considered.

As will be explained below, a registered fair rent cannot normally be altered for two years. It is unclear whether the prospects of inflation over the two-year period may be taken into account when the rent is initially determined.[4]

The result of excluding "personal circumstances" is that matters such as the financial situation of the particular landlord or tenant are irrelevant. In addition, it was held in *Mason* v. *Skilling*[5] that the fact that the tenant was a sitting tenant with security of tenure was a personal circumstance which could not affect the rent.

As far as the condition of the dwelling-house is concerned, it was held in *Williams* v. *Khan*[6] that the fair rent is not automatically nominal because the property is subject to a closing order on the basis that it is unfit for habitation. The closing order is only one factor, although an important one.

(b) *Matters to be disregarded*

By section 70(3), there shall be disregarded any disrepair or defect attributable to the failure of the tenant or any predecessor in title to comply with the terms of the regulated tenancy, and any

---

[2] *Ibid.* s.7.
[3] *Shaw* v. *Groom* [1970] 2 Q.B. 504.
[4] See Farrand and Arden, *Rent Acts and Regulations* (2nd ed.), p. 92.
[5] [1974] 1 W.L.R. 1437. See also *Palmer* v. *Peabody Trust* [1975] Q.B. 604 (absence of security no ground for rent reduction).
[6] (1982) 43 P. & C.R. 1. See [1980] Conv. 389–392 and [1981] Conv. 325–326 (J.T.F.) on the question whether the fixing of a nominal rent would have taken the tenancy out of protection as being at a rent less than two-thirds of the rateable value.

improvement carried out by the tenant or any predecessor in title,[7] other than pursuant to the terms of the tenancy. A similar principle applies to improvements to furniture or deterioration in its condition due to ill-treatment by the tenant or his lodger or sub-tenant.

Thus the fair rent is not to be decreased under section 70(1), where the state of repair is a relevant consideration, if the disrepair is attributable to the tenant. Nor does he have to pay more where he has enhanced the premises by improvements which he was not obliged to make.

(c) Scarcity[8]

Fundamental to the fair rent is section 70(2), whereby it is to be assumed that the number of persons seeking to become tenants of suitable dwelling-houses in the locality on the terms of the regulated tenancy is not substantially greater than the number of such dwelling-houses in the locality which are available for letting on such terms.

Thus the fair rent is less than a market rent because the scarcity element, which would otherwise increase the rent, is disregarded. Unlike the owner of other commodities, the owner of land cannot take advantage of shortages in order to increase the rent.

The manner in which the scarcity factor is eliminated is explained below. Before turning to the assessment of the rent, it should be emphasised that scarcity value must be distinguished from amenity value. In *Metropolitan Property Holdings Ltd.* v. *Finegold*[9] the amenity in question was an American school in St. John's Wood, which made the area desirable to American families, resulting in a shortage of accommodation. The tenant argued that this introduced a scarcity element, which should be disregarded. This argument was rejected: amenity advantages which increase the rent under section 70(1) do not result in a set-off under subsection (2) merely because the amenity attracts more people than can live in the area. Thus the rent will be higher if there are better amenities. The scarcity test should be applied over a substantial area, ignoring local scarcity caused by a particular amenity.

---

[7] See *Trustees of Henry Smith's Charity* v. *Hemmings* (1983) 265 E.G. 383 (Predecessor in title must have had the tenant's interest, therefore improvement not disregarded when done by predecessor before lease granted to him. It may suffice if done after the contract for the lease but before its grant).

[8] See generally [1985] Conv. 199 (P. Q. Watchman).

[9] [1975] 1 W.L.R. 349; (1975) 39 Conv. (N.S.) 295 (D. MacIntyre). *cf.* R.A. 1977, s.70(3)(c) and (d), repealed by H.A. 1980.

(*d*) *Methods of assessment of fair rents*

There is no obligation upon the rent officer (or, on appeal, the rent assessment committee) to adopt any particular method of assessing a fair rent. It has been held, however, that the best method is the consideration of comparables, *i.e.* the registered fair rents of comparable Rent Act tenancies in the locality. Unless recently registered, a higher sum should be fixed, to allow for inflation. In *Tormes Property Co. Ltd.* v. *Landau*[10] the rent assessment committee was held entitled to reject the landlord's figure, based on a return on the capital value, in favour of comparables. Little weight should be given to other methods when comparables were available. The landlord's calculation was a variation of the "contractor's theory," based on a return on building costs. This method, it was said, could do no more than set a ceiling for the rent. The landlord had estimated replacement costs, allowing reasonable interest and adding management expenses. This came to £5,000. A fair return of 8 per cent. led to a rent of £400 a year. This was increased to £565 by the addition of sums for insurance, equipment and so forth. The rent assessment committee did not criticise these figures, but declined to adopt this approach. The fair rent was fixed at £360, based on comparables. This figure, which gave a 4 per cent. return, was upheld. It has since been said by the House of Lords[11] that the "contractor's theory" is notoriously unreliable and is a method of last resort.

In the absence of comparables, a fair rent may be assessed by estimating the market rent and then making a reduction for scarcity. The problem here is that, as the volume of registered rents increases, it may be difficult to establish the hypothetical market rent. One approach is to calculate a fair return on the capital value. In *Mason* v. *Skilling*[12] the fair rent was assessed by looking at comparables and at the capital value with vacant possession. The tenant claimed that, as he was a sitting tenant, a lower figure should be taken, to reflect the absence of vacant possession. It held that the tenant's security was a "personal circumstance," to be disregarded under section 70(1). The higher figure was correct, as a fair rent must be fair to the landlord as well as the tenant: it must give him a fair return on his capital. Otherwise if there were two identical houses, one having a tenant with a wife and young children (potential successors to the tenancy) and the other being let to an elderly bachelor (with no successors), the capital values

[10] [1971] 1 Q.B. 261.
[11] In *Western Heritable Investment Co. Ltd.* v. *Husband, infra.*
[12] [1974] 1 W.L.R. 1437.

would be different, but it would be absurd if the rents were different. The rent assessment committee was entitled to have regard to the capital value as well as the comparables.

Where comparables are not the basis, the question arises as to how much should be deducted in order to achieve the disregard of the scarcity element. A figure of between 10 and 25 per cent. has often been stated, but a higher figure may be upheld. In *Western Heritable Investment Co. Ltd.* v. *Husband*[13] the House of Lords refused to interfere where 40 per cent. had been deducted for scarcity. The rent assessment committee which had fixed the rents now being relied on as comparables (and which were disputed as wrongly assessed) had found the capital value with vacant possession, applied 6 per cent. as a reasonable return, and then deducted 40 per cent. to reflect the severe scarcity in the area. Whether and how much to deduct was a question of fact to be determined on the evidence. It was difficult to demonstrate that the scarcity of rental accommodation inflated the vacant possession value, but this could reasonably be inferred, and therefore the deduction for scarcity was not erroneous. However, the rent may be fixed solely on the basis of comparables without considering a fair return on the capital, as comparables are the best guide.

(ii) The registration of a fair rent

The fair rent is determined by application to the rent officer. An appeal lies to the rent assessment committee, and thence to the High Court on a point of law.[14] Once ascertained, the rent will be registered. It then operates *in rem,* binding subsequent lettings of the dwelling-house, unless altered or cancelled, as explained below. It will cease to be operative, however, if it can be said that a subsequent letting is not of the same dwelling-house, for example, because there is a material difference in the extent of the property let.[15]

Application to the rent officer may be made by the landlord or the tenant, or by the parties jointly.[16] It may also be made by the

---

[13] [1983] 2 A.C. 849; [1985] Conv. 199 (P. Q. Watchman). The decision concerns the equivalent provisions of the Scottish legislation.

[14] By judicial review; *Ellis & Sons Fourth Amalgamated Properties Ltd.* v. *Southern Rent Assessment Panel* (1984) 270 E.G. 39.

[15] See *Gluchowska* v. *Tottenham Borough Council* [1954] 1 Q.B. 439; *cf. Solle* v. *Butcher* [1950] 1 K.B. 671. A mere change from unfurnished to furnished caused the registered rent to cease to be operative in *Kent* v. *Millmead Properties Ltd.* (1982) 44 P. & C.R. 353, which is doubted below, *post,* p. 145.

[16] R.A. 1977 s.67(1).

local authority,[17] to cover the case where the tenant may be reluctant, perhaps as a result of intimidation, to apply. The common reason today for local authority applications is because the tenant has applied to the authority for a rent allowance. In the case of joint landlords or joint tenants, it seems that an application by one alone is ineffective.[18]

Procedure before the rent officer is informal. The parties may be represented by lawyers or other persons. It is the usual practice to inspect the premises, although there is no obligation to do so.[19]

The application must be in prescribed form, and must specify the rent which the applicant seeks to register.[20] This is a mandatory requirement, so in *Chapman* v. *Earl*[21] the application was invalid where no figure was specified. Subject to that, the requirements are directory only, so that exact compliance is not essential. In *Druid Development Co. (Bingley) Ltd.* v. *Kay*[22] the landlord's application failed to give all the prescribed particulars. The existing rent was incorrectly stated, part of the premises (the garage) was omitted, and the husband was stated to be the tenant while in fact his wife was a joint tenant. The tenants took no objection and a rent was registered. It was held that they could not later claim that it was invalid. The requirements were directory, and nobody was misled. Either there was adequate compliance, or the inadequacy was waived. It was added that as applications are often made by laymen, a technical approach is to be discouraged.

Where the landlord or tenant alone applies, notice must be served on the other party, who may make representations. The rent officer may hold a consultation, at which the parties may be represented. After the decision, the parties are notified and can object within 28 days, whereupon the matter is referred to the rent assessment committee. If the application was a joint one, or if there were no representations, the rent officer will simply make his decision and notify the parties, although a consultation may be held.[23]

---

[17] *Ibid.* s.68. See *post*, p. 148. (restricted contracts).

[18] By analogy with *Turley* v. *Panton* (1975) 29 P. & C.R. 397 (restricted contract), *post*, p. 148.

[19] For further details, see Pettit, *Private Sector Tenancies* (2nd ed.), pp. 133 *et seq.*

[20] R.A. 1977, s.67(2). An application to re-register an *existing* rent is invalid; *R.* v. *Chief Rent Officer for Kensington and Chelsea L.B.C., ex p. Moberly*, (1986) 278 E.G. 305.

[21] [1968] 1 W.L.R. 135; *cf. R.* v. *London Rent Assessment Panel, ex p. Braq Investments Ltd.* [1969] 1 W.L.R. 970 (Valid where figure ascertainable, *e.g.* where a sum per square foot specified).

[22] (1982) 44 P. & C.R. 76.

[23] The procedure is set out in R.A. 1977, Sched. 11, as amended by H.A. 1980, Sched. 6.

In the case of a first registration, the rent officer's duty is to determine a fair rent and register it. If there is already a registered rent (which may be reconsidered according to rules explained below), he will either confirm the existing rent or register a different one.[24]

The amount registered is exclusive of rates, but if they are borne by the landlord (or superior landlord), that fact is noted on the register.[25] The amount registered, however, does include any sums payable for furniture or services, whether or not separate from the sums payable for occupation and whether or not payable under separate agreements.[26] Thus the landlord cannot evade full rent control by stipulating separate sums for "rent" and other matters.

Where, under the tenancy, the sums payable vary according to the cost of services or works of maintenance or repair, the amount registered as rent may be entered as a variable amount, if the rent officer (or rent assessment committee) is satisfied that the terms as to variation are reasonable.[27] If the rent officer is not so satisfied, he must assess the proper value to be attributed to services and include the amount in the fixed fair rent.[28] Where a variable rent is registered, the recoverable rent may accordingly be increased within the two-year period (during which registered rents cannot normally be increased) without reconsideration by the rent officer. Nor will the phasing rules, discussed below, apply. It has therefore been suggested that the rent officer should be cautious in accepting a variable rent, and that there should be a heavy onus upon the landlord to show that it is reasonable. It is not sufficient that the terms have been operated reasonably in the past; the terms themselves must be reasonable.[29]

Finally, the question when the registered rent takes effect must be considered. By section 72[30] of the 1977 Act, it takes effect from

---

[24] R.A. 1977, Sched. 11, para. 5.
[25] *Ibid.* s.71(2).
[26] *Ibid.* s.71(1).
[27] *Ibid.* s.71(4).
[28] *Firstcross Ltd.* v. *Teasdale* (1984) 47 P.& C.R. 228. See also *Wigglesworth* v. *Property Holding and Investment Trust PLC* (1984) 270 E.G. 555; *Betts* v. *Vivamat Properties Ltd.* (1984) 270 E.G. 849.
[29] Farrand and Arden, *Rent Acts and Regulations* (2nd ed.), pp. 98–99; (1983) 265 E.G. 286 (J. T. Farrand), criticising *Firstcross Ltd.* v. *Teasdale, supra.* See also [1983] Conv. 90 (J.T.F.), suggesting that where a variable rent is accepted, a rent exclusive of services should be registered, contrary to the usual practice.
[30] As substituted by H.A. 1980, s.61.

the date when registered by the rent officer or, if determined by a rent assessment committee, from the date of the committee's decision. If the current registered rent is confirmed, the confirmation takes effect from the date it is noted in the register by the rent officer, or, if confirmed by a rent assessment committee, from the date of its decision. This latter point is relevant to the question when the two-year period, during which further alterations cannot normally be made, begins to run. This is discussed below. In the case of a first registration, the effect of section 72 is that the tenant can be disadvantaged by any delay in the proceedings. If the rent finally registered is lower than his contractual rent, he cannot recover any excess for the period prior to the registration.[31] On a re-registration, on the other hand, the rent is normally increased, in which case the section operates to the tenant's advantage.[32]

(iii) Appeal to the rent assessment committee[33]

Either party, if dissatisfied with the rent officer's decision, may appeal to the rent assessment committee, from whose decision an appeal lies to court on a point of law. The rent assessment committee may require further information from the parties, and must serve notice on the parties specifying a period of not less than 14 days from the service of the notice during which representations may be made. If either party requests to make oral representations, he must be given an opportunity to be heard in person or by means of a lawyer or other person representing him. After making such inquiries it thinks fit, the rent assessment committee will confirm the rent registered or confirmed by the rent officer if it appears to be a fair rent, or, if it does not, determine a fair rent. The parties are then notified of the decision and its date.[34]

Once an appeal has been initiated, the appellant cannot withdraw the reference unilaterally, but the court can sanction the withdrawal if the parties agree and if it would not prejudice the public interest.[35] The public interest is involved because registra-

---

[31] Contrast the original s.72, whereby the registered rent took effect from the date of the application.

[32] See Farrand and Arden, *loc. cit.*, pp. 100–101.

[33] For the constitution of the committee, see R.A. 1977, Sched. 10.

[34] These provisions are found in R.A. 1977, Sched. 11, Part I. The committee may decide by a majority, although this fact will not be revealed. See *Picea Holdings Ltd.* v. *London Rent Assessment Panel* [1971] 2 Q.B. 216.

[35] *Hanson* v. *Church Commissioners for England* [1978] Q.B. 823. Contrast the position as to rent tribunals, *post*, p. 149.

tion affects neighbouring properties as a result of the fixing of fair rents by looking at comparables.

Rent assessment committees are subject to the rules of natural justice, and to the prerogative orders. They must give reasons for their decisions on request.[36] Questions have arisen as to the extent of this duty. Their reasons must be intelligible. They need not deal with every point raised, but must deal with substantial points. It was held in *Guppys (Bridport) Ltd.* v. *Knott (No. 3)*[37] that they need not state their methods of valuation. If they decide to rely on their own knowledge and experience, they are not further required to explain how their figures were reached, so long as they deal with the substantial points raised. This was taken further in *Waddington* v. *Surrey and Sussex Rent Assessment Committee,*[38] where the committee reduced the rent fixed by the rent officer, stating that they relied on what was found on inspection and on their own knowledge and experience. The landlord's appeal was allowed. The committee must deal with the evidence and, if it is rejected, explain why. Here no satisfactory reason was given for rejecting the next-door comparables.

A similar situation arose in *R.* v. *London Rent Assessment Committee, ex p. St. George's Court Ltd.,*[39] where the committee gave no explanation for rejecting comparables which were similar flats in the same block determined recently by another committee. The matter was remitted, to see if good reasons could be demonstrated. The reasons subsequently stated were that the tenants had not been represented before the other committee, and the evidence was therefore untested. This was taken to the Court of Appeal in *No. 2,*[40] and the decision quashed as showing an error of law. In effect, the committee was saying that the rent fixed by the other committee was not a fair rent, but it must be assumed to be right in law until shown to be wrong, for example, if cogent evidence or a significant argument was not before it.[41] In the case of a purpose-built block, the evidence must be very weighty to justify a departure from a recent fair rent.

Where the case of services is being considered, the committee,

---

[36] Tribunals and Inquiries Act 1971; Rent Assessment Committees (England and Wales) (Amendment) Regulations (S.I. 1981 No. 1783); [1979] Conv. 205 (P. Q. Watchman); [1983] Conv. 260 (J.T.F.).
[37] (1981) 258 E.G. 1083.
[38] (1982) 264 E.G. 717.
[39] (1983) 265 E.G. 984.
[40] (1984) 48 P. & C.R. 230. See also *Collins* v. *Murray* (1984) 271 E.G. 287.
[41] See also *Tormes Property Co. Ltd.* v. *Landau* [1971] 1 Q.B. 261.

as a basic principle, should give reasons if it rejects the landlord's figures. However, the committee is not obliged to use the costs as a basis, and has a discretion to look at the matter in some other way.[42]

(iv) Rent limit for protected tenancies

The basic principle is that the recoverable rent is the contractual rent. Even if a higher rent is registered, this is not recoverable during the protected tenancy. If, however, the landlord could give a notice to quit, a notice to increase the rent operates as a notice to quit, thus turning the tenancy into a statutory tenancy, governed by the rules explained below.[43]

The contractual rent cannot exceed any registered rent.[44] A landlord who charges a higher rent commits no offence, but the excess is recoverable by the tenant.[45] A protected tenant who is dissatisfied with his rent should, therefore, apply for the registration of a lower fair rent. Even if a higher figure is in fact registered, this is not recoverable during the protected tenancy, subject to the notice to quit rule.

It has already been stated that the registered rent is exclusive of rates. Where the rates are borne by the landlord, the rent limit is increased if there is an increase in the rates, so that the increase may be passed on to the tenant.[46]

Applying the principles of the law of contract, the parties should be free to increase the rent payable under the protected tenancy by agreement. In order to protect the tenant, however, a special rule applies, although it seems often to be ignored in practice. Where there is no registered rent, the rent under a protected tenancy may only be increased pursuant to a "rent agreement" satisfying the requirements of section 51.[47] The agreement must be in writing, signed by the parties. It must state that the tenant's security is not affected if he does not enter into the agreement; that if a rent were instead registered, any increase would be phased; and that the

---

[42] *R.* v. *London Rent Assessment Panel, ex p. Cliftvylle Properties Ltd.* (1983) 266 E.G. 44; *Perseus Property Co. Ltd.* v. *Burberry* (1985) 273 E.G. 405.

[43] R.A. 1977, s.49(4).

[44] *Ibid.* s.44(1).

[45] *Ibid.* ss.44(2), 57.

[46] *Ibid.* s.71(3). For the calculation of the rates, see Sched. 5.

[47] A "rent agreement" is also necessary if another regulated tenancy is granted to the tenant or person who might succeed him as statutory tenant; s.51(1)(*b*).

agreement does not prevent the parties from applying at any time for the registration of a fair rent. This statement must be at the head of the document, and must be in characters not less conspicuous than those used in any other part of the agreement.[48] Rent increased other than pursuant to such an agreement is not recoverable.[49] From the tenant's viewpoint, it is probably easier to apply for a registered rent.

Finally, special rules apply to determine the rent limit where the tenancy was brought into regulation by the Counter Inflation Act 1973,[50] and where the tenancy was converted from a controlled tenancy to a regulated tenancy.[51]

(v) Rent limit for statutory tenancies

If there is no registered rent, only the previous contractual rent is recoverable. If there is a registered rent, this may not be exceeded. If the registered rent is higher than the contractual rent, the rent may be increased up to the registered rent by a notice of increase in prescribed form.[52] Such a notice of increase may take effect in the middle of a rental period, the increase being apportioned.[53] Where the rates are borne by the landlord, any increase may be passed to the tenant without a notice of increase where the rent is registered.[54]

Where the rent is increased to the level of a higher registered rent by notice of increase, the whole of the increase is not immediately recoverable. The increase is phased so that, broadly speaking, only half of it is recoverable during the "period of delay," namely one year.[55] There is no phasing, however, of any increase attributable to an increase in the cost of services.

Where there is no registered rent, the rent limit during the statutory tenancy may be adjusted to take account of increases in rates

---

[48] See *Middlegate Properties Ltd.* v. *Messimeris* [1973] 1 W.L.R. 168.
[49] R.A. 1977, s.54.
[50] *Ibid*. Sched. 7.
[51] *Ibid*. s.52, introduced by H.A. 1980, s.68. An agreement purporting to increase the rent is void. The previous rent limit remains until a fair rent is registered.
[52] *Ibid*. s.45.
[53] *Avenue Properties (St. John's Wood) Ltd.* v. *Aisinzon* [1977] Q.B. 628.
[54] R.A. 1977, s.71(3). The rates are calculated according to Sched. 5. A notice of increase is required where there is no registered rent, as explained below.
[55] R.A. 1977, s.55, as amended by H.A. 1980, s.60. For an account of these complex rules, see Pettit, *Private Sector Tenancies* (2nd ed.), pp. 123 *et seq*.

or in the cost of providing furniture or services. In the case of furniture or services, the increase may be agreed in writing by the parties or determined by the county court.[56] In the case of rates, however, a notice of increase must be served, specifying the increase and the date from which it is to take effect.[57] It was held in *Aristocrat Property Investments Ltd.* v. *Harounoff*[58] that non-compliance cannot be waived by the tenant. There the landlord had demanded the increase by letter, and the tenant complied. A subsequent possession order based on arrears was erroneous, because the increase was not payable. The statutory requirements were mandatory. It was accepted, however, that there might be cases where the tenant's conduct might estop him from recovering amounts paid from the landlord.

Rent demanded in excess of the rent limit is not recoverable from the tenant, and amounts so paid are recoverable by him from the landlord.[59]

(vi) Alteration and cancellation of registered rents

(a) Alteration

A registered rent cannot be altered within two years unless the parties apply jointly, or unless there has been such a change in the condition of the dwelling-house, the terms of the tenancy, the quantity, quality or condition of any furniture, or any other circumstances taken into consideration previously, as to make the registered rent no longer a fair rent.[60] It is doubtful whether mere inflation is a change of circumstances within this provision. No doubt it was intended that the possibility of applying to increase the rent after two years without showing any change of circumstances would cater sufficiently for inflation.

If a change of circumstances to justify an application within two years is established, the rent may be reconsidered in the light of all the circumstances, not merely the change.[61] After the two-year

---

[56] R.A. 1977, s.47. It might be easier to apply for a registered rent.
[57] *Ibid.* s.46.
[58] (1982) 263 E.G. 352; [1983] Conv. 402 (J.E.M.).
[59] R.A. 1977, ss.45, 57.
[60] *Ibid.* s.67(3), as amended by H.A. 1980, s.60. By s.67(4), the landlord alone may apply within the last three months of the two-year period, but, by s.72, no alteration can take effect until the two years have expired. Where application is made within two years, but the registered rent is confirmed, it seems that the two year period starts afresh; s.67(5), as amended.
[61] *London Housing and Commercial Properties Ltd.* v. *Cowan* [1977] Q.B. 148.

period, the question has arisen whether the rent should merely be revised to take account of inflation. In *Kovats* v. *Corporation of Trinity House*[62] the tenant, appealing from the rent assessment committee on a point of law, claimed that the committee should have taken inflation alone into account, in the absence of a change of circumstances. It was held that section 70[63] applied to re-registrations as well as to first registrations. It was legitimate to consider the circumstances generally and to look at comparables. This is because rents do not necessarily increase precisely in step with inflation. But, of course, inflation must be a factor. So in *Wareing* v. *White*[64] the Court of Appeal held that the rent assessment committee had not acted improperly in looking at the Retail Price Index. The Committee had not suggested that rents must be rigorously kept in line with inflation. General inflation, amongst other things, could be considered, although increases in rents in the locality were of more assistance.

It might be expected that the re-letting of the premises on a furnished tenancy when the previous tenancy was unfurnished would be considered a change of circumstances justifying an increase in the rent.[65] It was held, however, in *Kent* v. *Millmead Properties Ltd.*[66] that the registered rent ceased to be operative in such a case. Hence the landlord, by re-letting on a furnished tenancy, could let at a higher rent. This seems inconsistent with the scheme of the Act, and it is noteworthy that the provisions on change of circumstances were not cited.

(b) Cancellation

The registered rent may be cancelled in two situations, so that a higher rent may be recovered. By section 73 of the 1977 Act, this is permissible on a joint application after the two-year period, where a "rent agreement"[67] has been entered into. The section has been extended by section 62 of the Housing Act 1980, so that the registered rent may also be cancelled after the two-year period where

---

[62] (1982) 262 E.G. 445.
[63] *Ante,* p. 134.
[64] (1985) 274 E.G. 488.
[65] See *Domo Investments Ltd.* v. *Dyer* (1978) 122 Sol.Jo. 421 (county court).
[66] (1982) 44 P. & C.R. 353; criticised [1983] Conv. 147 (F. Webb). The similar decision of the Court of Appeal in *Metrobarn Ltd.* v. *Gehring* [1976] 1 W.L.R. 776 is distinguishable as being based on the transitional provisions of R.A. 1974. The furnished tenancy there was pre-1974 and, therefore, not a regulated tenancy.
[67] *Ante,* p. 142.

there is currently no regulated tenancy, on the application of the person who would be the landlord if there were such a tenancy.

(vii) Certificates of fair rent

Where there is no registered rent, or where the rent was registered at least two years previously, and there is no current regulated tenancy, section 69[68] of the 1977 Act permits a person intending to let on such a tenancy to apply to the rent officer for a certificate of fair rent, specifying a rent which would be a fair rent under a regulated tenancy on such terms as are specified in the application. A certificate of fair rent may also be granted to a person intending to improve a dwelling-house, or to provide one by the erection or conversion of any premises. Where the certificate is issued, an application for registration of the rent may be made within two years of the date of the certificate.

The object of these provisions is to enable the landlord (or prospective landlord) to know what his position will be if he goes ahead with the letting, improvement or building, as the case may be. It has been criticised on the ground that the tenant is not there to make representations in the case of a prospective letting.[69]

(viii) Shorthold tenancies

As explained above, there is no requirement that the rent be registered in the case of an ordinary regulated tenancy. The position is otherwise in the case of shorthold tenancies, presumably to compensate for the lack of full security. It was originally provided that the tenancy could not be shorthold unless it had a registered rent, or a certificate of fair rent had been issued before the grant, followed by an application for registration not later than 28 days from the beginning of the term.[70] This requirement, however, now applies only if the dwelling-house is in Greater London.[71] Outside Greater London the tenant may, of course, still apply for the registration of a fair rent.

---

[68] The procedure is laid down in R.A. 1977, Sched. 12.
[69] The Francis Committee in 1971 recommended the abolition of certificates of fair rent; Report of the Committee on the Rent Acts (Cmnd. 4609, p. 64). This was not implemented, and, indeed, the certificate of fair rent has been given a role by the Housing Act 1980 in respect of shorthold tenancies, as explained below.
[70] H.A. 1980, s.52.
[71] Protected Shorthold Tenancies (Rent Registration) Order 1981 (S.I. 1981 No. 1578).

(ix) Jurisdiction

Clearly situations may arise where it is disputed whether a tenancy is a regulated tenancy. For example, it may be alleged that the tenancy is in fact a licence, or that it is a restricted contract, or a holiday letting. By section 141 of the 1977 Act, the county court has jurisdiction to determine whether a tenancy is protected or statutory, and what the rent limit is. It has no jurisdiction, however, to determine or alter a registered rent. So in *Tingey* v. *Sutton*,[72] where the tenant applied to the county court to set aside a rent registered by the rent officer, it was held that the court had no jurisdiction. The jurisdiction was that of the rent assessment committee, or, on appeal, the High Court.

Disputes as to jurisdiction arise not infrequently before the rent officer. Such was the case in *R.* v. *Rent Officer for Camden, ex p. Ebiri*,[73] where the tenant applied for a fair rent, but the landlord claimed that it was a holiday letting. The tenant started county court proceedings to determine the question of protection. Meanwhile the rent officer investigated the matter and was satisfied that it was not a holiday letting, but adjourned the matter *sine die*. The tenant succeeded in obtaining an order of mandamus to have the fair rent determined and registered. While the rent officer could not determine conclusively whether it was a protected tenancy, his duty was to consider the matter and inquire into the facts. If satisfied that the tenancy was protected, he was bound to proceed. He only had a discretion not to proceed if doubtful as to jurisdiction, or perhaps if he knew that the county court would decide the matter within 24 hours. If satisfied that it was not a protected tenancy, he should do nothing until the court held that it was. This, it is submitted, is satisfactory, in view of the rules relating to the date from which a registered rent takes effect, explained above. As the registered rent cannot take effect from a date prior to the registration, it would be undesirable if the tenant had to go on paying a high contractual rent until protracted court proceedings resolved the matter.

Restricted Contracts

In the absence of a registered rent, there is no restriction on the rent payable under a restricted contract, nor, as will be seen

---

[72] [1984] 1 W.L.R. 1154. See also *Druid Development Co. (Bingiey) Ltd.* v. *Kay* (1982) 44 P. & C.R. 76.
[73] [1982] 1 All E.R. 950; [1983] Conv. 403 (J.E.M.).

below, does the prohibition on premiums apply. Even if there is a registered rent, it has been held that there is no restriction on the rent payable under a restricted contract relating to part of the premises where the registered rent relates to the whole.[74]

By section 77 of the 1977 Act, either party to a restricted contract or the local authority may refer the contract to the rent tribunal. Before going any further it should be said that the rent tribunals were abolished by section 72 of the Housing Act 1980, whereby their functions were transferred to rent assessment committees, to be known as rent tribunals when carrying out these functions. The purpose of this apparently eccentric provision was to bring about uniformity in the method of appointment of members of rent tribunals and rent assessment committees from the same rent assessment panel.[75] In practice the same people sat on both bodies. The 1980 Act formalises that practice, thereby saving administrative expenses.

As explained in Chapter 8, the tenant's real motive in applying to the rent tribunal was often to benefit from the security of tenure which resulted from the application.[76] Since the repeal of the security provisions by the Housing Act 1980 (in respect of contracts entered into after that Act), a tenant who applies to the rent tribunal in the hope of achieving a rent reduction now runs the risk of an effective notice to quit, assuming a periodic tenancy. In the case of joint tenants (and, presumably, landlords), it has been held that all must jointly apply.[77] If one alone applied, there might be difficulties as to whether the others would be bound, and whether they could subsequently make applications. Although this seems inconsistent with the reasoning of *Lloyd* v. *Sadler*[78] (holding that one of joint tenants may alone become a statutory tenant), it is distinguishable on the basis that the departed tenant in *Lloyd* was not affected in any way by the acquisition of a statutory tenancy by the other.

Local authority applications were designed to deal with the case where the tenant might be reluctant, perhaps as a result of intimidation, to approach the rent tribunal. The local authority might

---

[74] *Gluchowska* v. *Tottenham Borough Council* [1954] 1 Q.B. 439. The tenant could, of course, seek a registered rent for his part in such a case.

[75] H.C., Standing Committee F, April 22, 1980, col. 2200; Farrand and Arden, *Rent Acts and Regulations* (2nd ed.), p. 338; [1980] Conv. 319–322 (J.T.F.).

[76] *Ante,* p. 114.

[77] *Turley* v. *Panton* (1975) 29 P. & C.R. 397; [1978] Conv. 436, at pp. 441–442 (J. Martin).

[78] [1978] Q.B. 774, *ante,* p. 65.

also be prompted by a tenant's application to the authority for a rent allowance. The local authority need not, of course, be a party to the restricted contract. Its application will be set aside if made in bad faith or if capricious, frivolous or vexatious, as where a "blanket reference" is made in respect of a block of flats without any investigation into the facts of individual cases.[79]

The reference to the rent tribunal is by written notice, containing certain particulars.[80] It is not, however, in prescribed form. These requirements are directory only, so that a reference which does not comply with them is not a nullity.[81] By section 78(1) the tribunal must consider any reference made to it, provided the reference is not withdrawn, as described below. The security consequences of the reference, in the case of contracts entered into before the Housing Act 1980, were explained in Chapter 8.

(i) Withdrawal of the reference

Section 78(1) imposes a duty on the rent tribunal to consider the reference unless it is withdrawn by the party who made it "before the tribunal have entered upon consideration of it." In *R.* v. *Tottenham Rent Tribunal, ex p. Fryer Bros. (Properties) Ltd.*[82] a reference was made by the tenant on October 8, and the hearing set for November 24. Before the hearing the landlord agreed to reduce the rent and so, on the evening of Friday, November 21, the tenant took a letter by hand to cancel the application. The offices were closed for the weekend, so the letter was put through the letterbox and opened on November 24. Meanwhile the members of the tribunal had taken the papers home over the weekend and read them. It was held that the notice of withdrawal was not properly served until it was communicated to the clerk of the tribunal during office hours. By then the members had already "entered upon consideration" of the reference. As the tribunal was an informal

---

[79] *R.* v. *Paddington and St. Marylebone Rent Tribunal, ex p. Bell London and Provincial Properties* [1949] 1 K.B. 666; *cf. R.* v. *Barnet and Camden Rent Tribunal, ex p. Frey Investments Ltd.* [1972] 2 Q.B. 342.

[80] Rent Assessment Committee (England and Wales) (Rent Tribunal) Regulations 1980 (S.I. 1980 No. 1700, as amended by S.I. 1981 No. 1493).

[81] *Francis Jackson Developments Ltd.* v. *Hall* [1951] 2 K.B. 488 (wrong lessor named). However, unless the wrong information is later corrected, the validity of the tribunal's decision will be affected; *R.* v. *Paddington and St. Marylebone Rent Tribunal, ex p. Haines* [1961] 1 Q.B. 388.

[82] [1971] 2 Q.B. 681.

body, it could do this without a meeting. Thus the withdrawal was too late, and the tribunal was entitled to continue. It appears that a reference can be withdrawn as of right until this stage, but thereafter not at all.[83]

(ii) How the rent tribunal proceeds

The tribunal is an informal body, its procedure being governed by statutory instrument.[84] The applicants may appear in person or be represented by lawyers or by other persons. Hearings are normally in public. The tribunal usually inspects the premises, although there is no statutory duty to do so. There is no power to take evidence on oath.[85] Strict rules of evidence do not apply, and the members are entitled to act on their own views, knowledge and experience.[86] The rules of natural justice apply, and the tribunal must give reasons for its decision on request, according to the Tribunals and Inquiries Act 1971. It has power to re-open a case, as where, for example, one party did not appear because he did not receive the notice of the hearing which was sent to him.[87] The tribunal has power to require information from the lessor, who commits an offence if he does not comply.[88]

The powers of the rent tribunal are set out in section 78(2) of the 1977 Act. After making such inquiry as it thinks fit and giving each party (and the housing authority if the general management of the dwelling is vested in it) an opportunity to be heard or of submitting written representations, the tribunal shall approve the rent payable under the contract, reduce or increase the rent to such sum as it thinks reasonable in all the circumstances, or dismiss the reference.[89] The parties are then notified of the decision. An approval, reduction or increase may be limited to a particular period.[90] The rent as approved, reduced or increased is then registered.[91] Where

---

[83] *Cf.* regulated tenancies, *ante,* p. 140.
[84] See n. 80, *supra.*
[85] *R.* v. *Fulham, Hammersmith and Kensington Rent Tribunal, ex p. Zerek* [1951] 2 K.B. 1.
[86] *R.* v. *Paddington North and St. Marylebone Rent Tribunal, ex p. Perry* [1956] 1 Q.B. 229. See generally [1980] Conv. 136 (C. Yates).
[87] *R.* v. *Kensington and Chelsea Rent Tribunal, ex p. Macfarlane* [1974] 1 W.L.R. 1486.
[88] R.A. 1977, s.77(2).
[89] It is not clear on what ground the power to dismiss is exerciseable; Farrand and Arden, *Rent Acts and Regulations* (2nd ed.), p. 111.
[90] R.A. 1977, s.78(4). This may allow a differential rent to be fixed; Farrand and Arden, *loc cit.,* p. 104.
[91] R.A. 1977, s.79.

the rent is altered, the alteration takes effect immediately, even before the date of registration.[92] There is no phasing of any increase.

As an anti-avoidance measure, section 85(3) provides that where the lessee pays separate sums for any two or more of (a) occupation, (b) use of furniture and (c) services, any reference in the statutory provisions to "rent" is a reference to the aggregate of those sums. If the sums are payable under separate contracts, the contracts are deemed to be one. Hence the landlord cannot diminish the rent tribunal's jurisdiction by denying the status of "rent" to certain sums paid by the tenant.[93]

(iii) The "reasonable" rent

Unlike regulated tenancies, where the concept of the "fair" rent applies, section 78(2) introduces the word "reasonable" as characterising the rent payable under a restricted contract. No specific guidelines are laid down in the Act as to what is meant by "reasonable," in contrast to the detailed provisions of section 70 in relation to a fair rent.[94] The rent tribunal must, however, consider "all the circumstances," which must certainly include matters such as the age, character, locality and state of repair of the dwelling. It is not clear how far the scarcity element is to be disregarded. It is generally assumed that a "reasonable" rent is broadly similar to a "fair" rent, but rents under restricted contracts are normally higher than those payable under comparable regulated tenancies. If scarcity was not to be disregarded, and hence a market rent payable, it is difficult to see any point in the rent control provisions. As the registered rents tend to be lower than market rents, it would seem that the scarcity element is disregarded to some extent.[95] Another difficulty is whether the tribunal should disregard the "personal circumstances" of the parties, as must be done in the case of a fair rent under section 70. The different wording of the two provisions suggests that personal circumstances are not irrelevant to a "reasonable" rent, but it is submitted that they should be disregarded. The registered rent, as explained below, operates *in rem*, binding the parties' successors in title. Although the registered rent is subject to reconsideration on a change of cir-

---

[92] *Villa D'Este Restaurant Ltd.* v. *Burton* [1957] 1 Q.B. 214 (Increase). It is not clear whether the alteration can be retrospective.
[93] See also s.79(3) as to rates.
[94] *Ante,* p. 134.
[95] See Farrand and Arden, *loc cit.*, pp. 109–110.

cumstances, it would seem odd that the personal circumstances of one party should affect the rent payable by his successor.

(iv) The effect of registration

Registration operates *in rem,* affecting restricted contracts entered into subsequently in respect of the same dwelling-house, until such time as the registration is altered or cancelled, as explained below. Where there is a registered rent, it is unlawful for any person to require or receive a higher rent. The person committing the offence is liable to a fine or imprisonment or both, and the excess rent is recoverable by the person who paid it.[96] However, criminal proceedings may only be instituted by the local authority, and are apparently rare.

(v) Reconsideration and cancellation of the registered rent

By section 80(1) of the 1977 Act, either party or the local authority may refer to the tribunal for a reconsideration of the registered rent. Save in the case of a joint application by the lessor and lessee, this cannot be done within the period of two[97] years since the rent was last considered by the tribunal, except on the ground that, since that date, there has been such a change in the condition of the dwelling, the furniture or services provided, the terms of the contract, or any other circumstances taken into account when the rent was last considered, as to make the registered rent no longer reasonable.

The possibility of cancellation was introduced by section 71 of the Housing Act 1980, providing that a registered rent may be cancelled after two years where the dwelling is not presently subject to a restricted contract, on the application of the person who would be the lessor if there were such a contract. The lessor is then free to enter into a new restricted contract at a higher rent, but the tenant can, of course, refer the rent to the rent tribunal.

(vi) Jurisdiction[98]

In the event of a dispute as to whether a restricted contract exists, section 141 of the 1977 Act gives the county court jurisdiction to determine the matter. Usually, however, the matter will be raised before the rent tribunal, in which case the tribunal must

---

[96] R.A. 1977, s.81.
[97] Reduced from 3 by H.A. 1980, s.70.
[98] See generally (1977) 41 Conv. (N.S.) 379 (P. H. Pettit).

decide whether it has jurisdiction.[99] Its decision, of course, is not conclusive. If the dispute involves a point which the tribunal is not competent to deal with, the proceedings should be adjourned to court. If the rent tribunal decides that it has jurisdiction, it will proceed with the matter, but the dissatisfied party may have the question of jurisdiction determined by the county court.

Finally, where the restricted contract relates to part only of premises which have been rated as a whole, and no apportionment of the rateable value has been made, section 82 gives the rent tribunal jurisdiction to deal with the reference if it appears to them that they would have had jurisdiction had the apportionment been made, unless the lessor in the course of the proceedings requires an apportionment and brings proceedings in the county court for that purpose within two weeks.

Illegal Premiums

The restrictions discussed above upon the rent recoverable under a regulated tenancy or a restricted contract would not serve their purpose if premiums, *i.e.* capital sums, could be required on the grant or assignment of the tenancy. It is accordingly unlawful to require a premium on the grant or assignment of a regulated tenancy or, in certain cases, in respect of a restricted contract.

It will be appreciated that such premiums are illegal only if the tenancy is within the Rent Act. A premium is, of course, perfectly lawful on the grant of a long lease at a ground rent, where the Rent Act does not apply because the rent is less than two-thirds of the rateable value. Landlords may not, however, take advantage of this principle in the case of a short lease by charging a premium and ground rent if the arrangement is a sham device to evade the Act. In *Samrose Properties Ltd.* v. *Gibbard*[1] property was let for a year for a lump sum of £35 and a rent of £1 quarterly. The object was to prevent the Rent Act from applying because the rent was less than two-thirds of the rateable value. It was held that the property had in effect been let at a rent of £39 for the year, so that the Act applied.

(i) The meaning of "premium"

The definition of "premium" in section 128(1) of the 1977 Act includes "any fine or other like sum" and "any other pecuniary

---

[99] *R.* v. *Croydon and South West London Rent Tribunal, ex p. Ryzewska* [1977] 1 Q.B. 876.
[1] [1958] 1 W.L.R. 235. See also *Woods* v. *Wise* [1955] 2 Q.B. 29.

consideration in addition to rent." This definition left it unclear whether a returnable deposit, for example to cover breakages or arrears of rent, was included.[2] The matter was resolved by the Housing Act 1980, section 79, providing that the definition includes any sum paid by way of a deposit, other than one which does not exceed one-sixth of the annual rent and is reasonable in relation to the potential liability in respect of which it is paid.

It is likely that a payment by the tenant of the landlord's costs in relation to the grant of the tenancy will constitute a premium.[3] The premium rules also cover the case where a loan (secured or unsecured) is required to be made on the grant or assignment of the tenancy.[4]

(ii) The grant of a protected tenancy

By section 119(1) of the 1977 Act, any person who, as a condition of the grant, renewal or continuance of a protected tenancy, requires in addition to the rent the payment of any premium, shall be guilty of an offence. Similarly any person who, in connection with the grant, renewal or continuance of a protected tenancy, receives any premium in addition to the rent.[5] In addition to imposing a fine, the court may order the repayment of the premium.[6]

The premium need not be paid to the landlord himself. Thus in *Elmdene Estates Ltd.* v. *White*[7] the offence was committed where the landlord required the tenant to sell his house to a third party at £500 below the market price as a condition of the grant of a tenancy of a flat. This was in effect a premium of £500.

While section 119 is directed primarily at landlords, the offence may be committed by "any person." So in *Farrell* v. *Alexander*[8] the section applied where the tenant surrendered the tenancy to the landlord on the basis that the landlord would grant a new tenancy to X, the tenant taking a premium from X. A premium paid on a direct assignment to X would be caught by section 120,

---

[2] See *R.* v. *Ewing* (1977) 65 Cr.App.R. 4.
[3] *Hansard,* H.L., Vol. 411, col. 585.
[4] R.A. 1977, ss.119(1), 120(1). Any sum lent is repayable on demand; s.125(2).
[5] *Ibid.* s.119(2).
[6] *Ibid.* s.119(3), (4); Criminal Justice Act 1982, ss.35–46.
[7] [1960] A.C. 528.
[8] [1977] A.C. 59, (1977) 41 Conv. (N.S.) 61 (D. MacIntyre). This decision closed a loophole in the Act; see *Zimmerman* v. *Grossman* [1972] 1 Q.B. 167, overruled by *Farrell* v. *Alexander.*

discussed below, but the argument that section 119 was confined to landlords was rejected.

(iii) The assignment of a protected tenancy

Similar conditions to those discussed above apply to the assignment of a protected tenancy. By section 121, it is an offence to require or receive a premium as a condition of, or in connection with the assignment. Although directed primarily at assigning tenants, the offence, as in the case of section 119, may be committed by "any person." Certain payments may, however, properly be required by the assignor. These are dealt with by section 120(3), and include payments in respect of outgoings paid by the assignor which are referable to a period after the assignment, and sums not exceeding the amount of any expenditure reasonably incurred by the assignor in carrying out alterations to the dwelling-house or in providing or improving fixtures.

These rules are confined to protected tenancies because statutory tenancies are not generally assignable. A statutory tenancy may, however, be assigned by an agreement to which the landlord is a party, but no pecuniary consideration may be required in such a case.[9] Where a statutory tenant gives up possession, he commits an offence if he requests or receives payment or other consideration from any person other than the landlord.[10]

(iv) Excessive price for furniture

The premium rules could, of course, be flouted if, instead of asking for a capital sum, the landlord or assigning tenant could achieve the same result by asking excessive prices for furniture and fixtures. To avoid such a possibility, section 123 provides that where the purchase of any furniture[11] is required as a condition of the grant, renewal, continuance or assignment of a protected tenancy or of rights under a restricted contract,[12] then if the price exceeds the reasonable price of the furniture, the excess is a premium. Local authorities have draconian powers in relation to the enforcement of these provisions,[13] but it is thought that the offence is commonly committed.

---

[9] R.A. 1977, Sched. 1, paras. 13, 14.
[10] *Ibid.* para. 12.
[11] Defined by s.128(1) as including fittings and other articles.
[12] The section applies only to restricted contracts where there is a registered rent; s.122(1).
[13] S.124.

An example of the operation of this rule is *Farrell* v. *Alexander,*[14] where £4,000 was required for furniture and fittings, which were worth much less. Similarly *Ailion* v. *Spiekermann,*[15] where the prospective assignee agreed to pay £3,750 for certain chattels, which, it was claimed, were worth only about £600. Specific performance was ordered of the contract to assign the tenancy and to transfer the chattels at a reasonable price.[16]

(v) Advance payments

These are prohibited by section 126, providing that where a protected tenancy is granted, continued or renewed, any requirement that rent shall be payable before the beginning of the rental period in respect of which it is payable shall be void whether imposed as a condition of the grant or under its terms. Similarly void is any requirement that rent shall be payable more than six months before the end of the rental period in respect of which it is payable (if that period is more than six months). The consequence of such a "prohibited requirement" is that the rent for any rental period to which it relates is irrecoverable from the tenant. A fine may be imposed, and any rent paid in compliance with the prohibited requirement may be ordered to be repaid.[17]

In *R.* v. *Ewing*[18] it was held that a payment by cheque the day before the start of the first rental period did not fall within the prohibition, as the cheque had to be cleared. It might be otherwise, however, in the case of a cash payment.

(vi) Allowable premiums

The situation may arise where a tenant lawfully pays a premium on the grant or assignment of a tenancy which is not within the Rent Act. Subsequently the tenancy becomes protected, so that the tenant would suffer hardship if he could not charge a premium on assignment. To alleviate his position, premiums may lawfully be charged in such cases. This could arise where the rent, initially less than two-thirds of the rateable value, has risen above that limit

---

[14] *Supra.*

[15] [1976] Ch. 158. For an unusual case where £40,000 was held lawful, see *Nock* v. *Munk* (1982) 263 E.G. 1085 (luxury flat done out by professional interior decorator).

[16] For guidance on the meaning of "reasonable price," see *Eales* v. *Dale* [1954] 1 Q.B. 539.

[17] See R.A. 1977, s.126(5) to (9), for further details.

[18] (1977) 65 Cr.App.R. 4. Compare *Official Solicitor to the Supreme Court* v. *Thomas, The Times,* March 3, 1986 (rent for agricultural holding not paid when landlord receives cheque).

because of an increase in the service charge element.[19] Or the tenancy might have been brought into protection after its grant by legislation such as the Counter-Inflation Act 1973, or by section 73 of the Housing Act 1980, amending in certain cases the rule that a tenancy cannot be protected if the landlord's interest belongs to the Crown.

Space does not permit an examination here of the detailed provisions applicable in such cases.[20]

(vii) Restricted contracts

The prohibitions on premiums apply on the grant or assignment of rights under restricted contracts only where a rent has been registered. As in the case of protected tenancies, sums may properly be required in respect of outgoings discharged by the grantor or assignor relating to the period after the grant or assignment.[21]

(viii) Effect of the premium rules

As already stated, infringement of the rules constitutes a criminal offence, and any premium paid is recoverable by the person who paid it.[22]

It remains to consider the civil law position where a contract has been made which includes a term for the payment of an illegal premium. In *Ailion* v. *Spiekermann*[23] a tenant contracted to assign for an illegal premium. It having become apparent that the premium could not be enforced, the assignor sought to avoid performing the contract by claiming that it was void for illegality. It was held that the contract as a whole was not illegal. The bad part could be severed, and specific performance granted of the contract to assign without the premium. After all, if the issue of illegality had been raised only after performance of the contract, the premium would be recoverable. But specific performance is a discretionary remedy. It might not be awarded where the assignor was ignorant and the assignee "tempted him with a cheque book," or where the assignor changed his mind before the assignee had altered his

---

[19] *i.e.* in cases where the service element is not disregarded under R.A. 1977, s.5(4).
[20] See R.A. 1977, ss.121, 127 and Sched. 18; H.A. 1980, Sched. 8; Pettit, *Private Sector Tenancies* (2nd ed.), pp. 258–261, 265–268; (1986) 83 L.S.G. 19 (R. Stapylton–Smith).
[21] R.A. 1977, s.122.
[22] *Ibid.* s.125(1).
[23] *Supra;* (1976) 40 Conv. (N.S.) 379 (D. MacIntyre). See also *Rees* v. *Marquis of Bute* [1916] 2 Ch. 64.

position in reliance on the contract. In normal circumstances, how-ever, the contract will be specifically enforced. The assignee is not precluded from seeking this remedy even though he knew of the illegality, because the statutory provisions were designed for his protection.

INDEX